Starting Off Right in Torts

Starting Off Right in Torts

SECOND EDITION

Carolyn J. Nygren
Howard E. Katz

Carolina Academic Press
Durham, North Carolina

Library of Congress Cataloging-in-Publication Data

Nygren, Carolyn, 1942–
Starting off right in torts / Carolyn J. Nygren and Howard E. Katz. — 2nd ed.
p. cm. — (Carolina Academic Press starting off right series)
ISBN 978-1-59460-829-2 (alk. paper)
1. Torts—Study and teaching—United States. 2. Law—Study and teaching—United States. I. Katz, Howard E. II. Title. III. Series.

KF1250.N94 2011
346.7303071'1—dc22 2011013634

Carolina Academic Press
700 Kent Street
Durham, NC 27701
Telephone (919) 489-7486
Fax (919) 493-5668

Printed in the United States of America
2021 Printing

Contents

Preface · How to Use This Book vii
Introduction · The Study of Torts Is Unique xiii

Chapter 1 · Information Necessary for Law School Survival 3
Case Reading — A Time-Consuming Task 3
1. Cases were not written as teaching materials 3
2. Cases are full of words you don't know 4
Casebooks — A Mystery 5
1. The cases in your casebook are from many jurisdictions 5
2. Casebook editors often try to "hide the ball" 6
The Ultimate Goal 7
Taking Notes on Cases — Briefs? 7
Cases and Classes 10
Note Taking — Keeping the Goal in Mind 11
More About What Happens in Class 12
Outlining — Perfection Not Needed 13
Law School Testing — A Shock 16
Grading — More Mystery 18
Exam Answers — Need for Practice 20
Practicing the Method 23

Chapter 2 · Intentional Torts 25
Battery 26
Case Reading and Note Taking 26
Test Taking and Grading 33
Sample Question 39
Assault 44
Analysis Hints 44
Sample Question with Answer 46
Practice Questions 47

False Imprisonment 52
Sample Question 52
Intentional Infliction of Severe Emotional Distress 54
Sample Question 55

Chapter 3 · Negligence 59
Analysis Hints 59
The Two Meanings of "Negligence" 59
Note: Proximate Cause vs. Legal Cause 60
No Duty to Act 61
Special Policy Considerations 64
Sample Questions 68
Duty and Standard of Care 69
Breach 72
Inferring Negligence — Negligence per se 75
Cause in fact 78
Legal (Proximate) Cause 81
Practice Questions 84
Breach 84
Inferring Breach — Res Ipsa Loquitur 86
Legal (Proximate) Cause 88
Multiple Parties 91

Chapter 4 · Strict Liability and Products Liability 95
Analysis Hints 95
Draft Outline 98
Draft Outline: Products Liability 99
Sample Questions 101
Abnormally Dangerous Activity 101
Manufacturing Defect 103
Design Defect 105
Practice Question 108

Chapter 5 · Multi-Issue Torts Questions 113

Chapter 6 · Confronting Your Final Exam 123
Torts Checklist 124
Using Old Exams to Prepare 125
Final Thoughts 127

Preface

How to Use This Book

This book is designed to provoke thought and discussion, not provide answers. It will suggest organization, analysis and writing techniques helpful to you from the first day of class. As you become more sophisticated in your knowledge of the law, your analysis and writing skills will also become more sophisticated. This book can only give you a foundation. But it is our hope that by providing you with that foundation, everything you do in your first weeks and months of law school will be done with greater purpose and direction. Nevertheless, we encourage you to change our rule statements and listings of elements, create your own methods of organizing the material, challenge our analysis of the facts, add philosophical and policy considerations, and even come to different conclusions. In order to help you, the methods we suggest have to be seen as a starting point which is then adapted to your needs and to the expectations of your professors.

The book starts with a short introduction entitled "The Study of Torts is Unique" that discusses how studying torts is different from studying any other course. Chapter One discusses information necessary for law school survival. A version of Chapter One appears in every book in this series except Civil Procedure (with each version having examples from the subject matter of the particular book). If you have already read the first chapter in another one of the books in the series, you may want to skip over Chapter One and go right to Chapter Two on intentional torts if that's where your course starts. If you have not yet covered intentional torts in class, you should still read the section on battery in Chapter Two for the important skills components it addresses, and then proceed to the topics in the book you have covered in your class.

The tort of battery in Chapter Two is followed by sections on some of the other intentional torts. We have not covered all of them, and we have spent very little time on defenses (but the same step-by-step approach we set out for the intentional torts we do cover can be applied to other topics as well). We also have not covered defamation. Although it can sometimes be an intentional tort, most professors either cover defamation at the end of the course or not at all.

Chapter Three is a long chapter on negligence. Your professor is likely to devote substantially more time to negligence than to intentional torts. Therefore, we have tried to point out many problem areas. Chapter Four covers strict liability and products liability. Chapter Five addresses multiple issue fact patterns, with suggestions about how to practice handling the organizational problems of torts exams. Chapter Six provides some specific hints on how to approach your final exams (though of course the entire book sets out an approach to outlining and answer-writing that is designed to improve your exam performance).

This book is not designed to teach you the law. Although most students find that they need more than their casebooks and class notes to learn the rules of law, your bookstore already is full of various commercial outlines and hornbooks to explain the law. We have found that almost all students learn more than enough law. What many students find difficult is learning what to do with all that substantive knowledge, and how to organize what they know in a usable way. That is the focus of this book. Assuming you know the law, this book will enable you to demonstrate your knowledge on an exam.

Each chapter begins with an explanation of useful techniques used to approach problems in a particular torts topic. This will be followed by a draft outline of the topic. The draft outline consists of basic rule statements, usually in the form of a listing of elements. It is suggested that you insert the information you've learned from the cases, your class, and any outside sources about how these rules have been interpreted. The rules in torts have been centuries in the making and no two people would state them in exactly the same way. If you have looked at more than one commercial outline or hornbook, you will find that the statements of any given rule differ. What's worse, even if you have a case in your casebook where the court states a rule, it may not be precisely the same as in another case or in a hornbook. Unfortunately, the judges who decided the cases in your book and who wrote the opinions did not have your understanding of torts in mind when they wrote those opinions. Do not let any of this disturb you. The basic elements of the rules probably are similar in any of these sources. Because there is no one authoritative phrasing of the rules, one is usually free to compose a rule that makes sense as long as it contains the accepted elements. Of course if your professor gives you a particular rule statement, you would be very wise to use it. Each chapter will also include sample exam questions, sample notes for an answer, and some sample answers.

These books are designed to give you organizational strategies for answers to exam questions, not a complete explanation of every rule and every doctrine.

These books are particularly good for study group use. If you are part of a study group, you might want to turn to Chapter Six to read the suggestions of how study groups can work on exam preparation. The material in each of the chapters can be used throughout the semester as your group meets, or near the end of the semester as you begin to review.

The approach we suggest attempts to insure that a student addresses all the issues in an exam question. We explain below and again in the section on battery how to answer a question by first doing a "top-down" analysis—going step by step through each element or sub-element that applies to a particular tort or defense. Then we suggest that you proceed "bottom up", looking more closely at each fact in the question to make sure you have not missed its possible significance. At some point before you begin actually writing your exam answer (either after you have done your top-down analysis, or after you have done both the top-down and bottom-up analysis) we suggest you underline or cross out the words in the fact pattern that you have used in your notes. You should then look at the words not crossed out to see if you have missed something important. Sometimes words you have not crossed out are there only to advance the story of the fact pattern. But sometimes they may prompt you to notice a major issue you may have missed. So why not cross those words out the first time you use them? Because sometimes the same fact can fit into your answer in more than one place. Going step by step (top down) and then focusing more closely on facts and crossing out words in a fact pattern (bottom up) are important exam techniques for many students. However, these are not techniques that can be successfully employed for the first time during an actual exam. They require practice. We therefore provide the opportunity to practice in each chapter.

Here is one suggested way to use the book:

After each sample answer there is a copy of the question. We provide a second copy of the question because most law students seem compelled to underline words in a question the first time they read it. This way you will have a clean copy of the question when you practice giving your own answer, including the method of identifying important words. We suggest that you read the Notes for Answer and then the sample answer as many times as necessary in order to follow our approach. Then read the copy of the question. First apply the top-down method of reading the facts given and determining what tort or torts are likely to be involved. Then for each arguable tort, try to recall everything you know about it. That means the elements, of course, but it also means anything else you learned about an element or the tort in the course. Once you have outlined all of this—the things the legal system considers relevant for that tort, and thus the things that must be demonstrated—you then apply the facts to the existing rules, elements, policy, etc. Then, after having done this top-down analysis, taking what you already know about a tort and seeing if the facts of this case demonstrate it, you should use the bottom-up approach. This means taking another close look at each fact given, underlining or crossing out the words from the question that we used in our suggested answer or that you used in your top-down draft of an answer. Using the notes you have from your reading of cases and from class, see if there are any issues or sub-issues we did not include in our Notes for Answer and Sample Answer, and add those to your analysis. Although legal doctrines will be similar in any given sources, the cases you have read or the notes you have taken may modify what we have said, and obviously should be taken into account. After you have added to the Notes for Answer, put the book answer out of sight. Put the question with the underlinings you have made and your modified notes in front of you. Write out your own answer to the question—taking as much time as you need to be satisfied with your work. Then you may want to write the answer again, but using less time. We have left some questions without answers so that you can practice on your own or with a study group.

Most professors do not provide a format for a model exam answer. We are suggesting a generic format that can be adapted to fit most classes. If your professor gives you an answer format that differs, obviously that is the one you should use.

Chapter Six is meant to be read now and shortly before your final exam. This book cannot prepare you for every question asked by every professor. Rather, its purpose is to provide you with a deliberate approach and the building blocks of answers so that you can construct your own answers. Chapter Six contains suggestions for exam preparation (including a checklist of torts issues) and some hints for strategizing during your actual exam.

In a law school exam situation you will need to spend from one third to one half of the time allotted for each question in thinking and planning, because the questions will be complex. Once you have done so, you must be able to compose your answer and write it out quickly. Exam writing is a skill, and as with any other skill, good results are achieved by practice. Although practicing writing and rewriting simple answers may seem mundane, the time is well spent. The more complicated questions in the law school exam are usually no more than a combination of simpler questions similar to those you will find in this book.

You can expect this book to help you in four ways:

1. We give you draft outlines so that you don't have to agonize over starting your own.
2. We provide techniques for reading fact patterns successfully.
3. We make suggestions for how to organize your answers coherently on exams, using a step-by-step approach.
4. We supply sample questions and suggested answers for each topic so you can practice your writing.

Your feedback is welcome. Please email comments and suggestions to Howard Katz, hkatz@elon.edu.

Introduction

The Study of Torts Is Unique

The organization of the traditional torts casebook is usually pretty straightforward. That makes torts a unique course, as it is sometimes very difficult to see the organizing principles in other courses. The organization helps the novice law student learn the complexities of legal analysis logically and gradually. Most, but not all, torts courses start with intentional torts. It is easy to understand imposing liability on someone for causing harm to someone else intentionally. Of course you will soon see that intent can mean something fuzzier than conscious desire, but intentional torts are still fairly clear, and lend themselves well to element-by-element analysis. The next topic—negligence—is perceived by students as somewhat more murky. Negligence imposes liability, not for our intentional acts, but for our failures to take proper care to prevent harm that we should be able to foresee. Where the creation of risk is overt, this still makes a lot of sense. But as the cases and your professor cause you to wrestle with just what should be considered a foreseeable harm, you are likely to feel things have gotten mushier. This is where the discipline of a step-by-step analysis will really begin to pay off, even if there is no one right answer. The final point along the fault spectrum—strict liability—is limited in most modern courts to a few specific situations, and will probably seem clearer than negligence. A related topic—products liability—will have aspects of negligence and aspects of strict liability to it, and so it can also serve as a review or second look at some of the doctrines discussed earlier in the course, with a heavy dose of policy added in (as most professors teach it).

Some casebooks do not follow this sequence. If your casebook and course start with negligence, it may help you to get the bigger picture of torts if you think of negligence in the middle of a continuum of fault-based tort liabilities (from intentional to negligent to strict liability).

Starting Off Right in Torts

Chapter 1

Information Necessary for Law School Survival

Case Reading—A Time-Consuming Task

You will spend a lot of your time in law school reading cases. Although much of the law is made by legislatures, judges also make law. And in the first year of law school judge-made law (the common law) is the primary raw material studied. These common-law rules have evolved over centuries, and are the source of the basic rules in contracts, property, and torts. As a lawyer, one of the important tasks you will have to perform is determining the law that governs a particular situation. Sometimes this will merely require looking at a statute. But at other times you will have to read one or more cases to determine the governing rule. Therefore, one of the most important skills you should learn in law school is how to read cases. The problem is that cases are very hard to read, for at least two reasons:

1. Cases were not written as teaching materials

You may be accustomed to college textbooks written by authors whose goal it was to help you to understand the subject matter. These textbooks may start out with introductory material and progress from the easy topics to the difficult ones. They will often have summaries, lists of important factors, and other guides to make the text more understandable. Textbook authors have editors who improve the readability of the manuscript. On the other hand, cases are written by judges for lawyers. They are not written to help you as a student. Judges are not always concerned with the clarity of their writing because they are writing for lawyers who already are familiar with the legal issues. Although casebook editors may edit or omit some sections of the cases they use, they do not change the language of the judge, nor do they correct what was written to make sure it agrees with other cases or with the casebook author's approach.

2. Cases are full of words you don't know

You will learn some of this puzzling vocabulary later in the year in your Civil Procedure course, but that is of little help to you now. Some of the vocabulary is specific to a given subject area of law, so you will learn it as the course moves along, but that too is of little help to you the first time you encounter a term. Very few law schools spend any time teaching this vocabulary to you at the beginning of the year. So you will have to learn it yourself. Unfortunately, the time you spend trying to understand this vocabulary is time you could spend thinking about legal analysis, but without the vocabulary, it will be impossible to move on to analysis.

Most cases you will read are appellate case decisions, and formal requirements must be met before any case can be appealed. Some of the difficult vocabulary arises from the fact that the losing party must cite an error that the judge made during the trial that, if not made, would have resulted in the case being decided in its favor.

You will see as you read the cases that there are only a few types of errors made by lower court judges that can give rise to a successful appeal. In some cases the judge stopped the trial and the losing party is appealing the fact that it never got a complete trial—motion to dismiss; motion on the pleadings; motion for summary judgment; judgment as a matter of law (formerly called motion for directed verdict). Other errors do not involve stopping the trial. Instead, the attorney for the losing side objected to the judge's ruling on a question of law at the time of the trial. This can be a ruling concerning evidence, or it can be a claim that the judge gave the jury an improper or inaccurate instruction as to the governing law of the case. Finally, two other types of errors occur after the verdict has been given by the jury (if there is one): denial of a motion for a new trial, and renewal of motion for judgment after trial (formerly called motion for judgment notwithstanding the verdict).

These claimed errors are called the "procedural issues" in appellate cases. You may see a sentence such as, "The only issue in this case is whether the trial judge erred in granting the motion to dismiss." Do not let this slow down your reading. Having a procedural issue is a legal formality, but it has little if anything to do with the reason why you are reading the case in your torts course. You are reading the case for the rule of tort law at stake—what the law is and how it applies to the facts in the case. These are often referred to as the "substantive issues." The substantive issue in your case may be, "Does the fact that Jane is only six years old mean that she is not able to form the intent necessary to be found liable for battery?" It is unlikely you will need to master the procedural issues as you read the case, though your professor may spend some time on them, and may even ask you to include them in your class recitation. The most important thing to be aware of procedurally is whether there was actually a trial in the case (which means the fact finder heard all the facts) or whether the case was decided before there was a trial. The other thing to be aware of (and this is related to the previous aspect of the case) is whether the appellate court is announcing which party wins the case, or whether the appellate court is merely telling the lower court (and us) what the rule of law is, and now giving the parties a chance to prove whether or not the facts fit that rule (and thus determine who wins and loses).

Casebooks—A Mystery

Although some casebooks are superb, others leave students confused. It would be reasonable for you to expect that your casebooks will help you learn the skill of reading cases as well as the law of torts. Unfortunately, few if any casebooks will give you that help. Some casebook editors seem to assume that you are able to understand how to read cases without instruction. They also assume that you will be able to learn both a rule of law and the skill of legal problem solving just from the cases you read. But most standard casebooks make this nearly impossible.

Somewhere there may be a person who learned the legal rules necessary to the study of law solely from a casebook, but your authors have never met anyone who did. So, in desperation, students reach for one of the many commercial study aids that fill shelf after shelf at the law school bookstore. While there is nothing wrong with commercial outlines as such, they can be dangerous if a student relies exclusively on them. But it is not uncommon to hear about students who literally go semester after semester without even buying the casebooks for class.

1. The cases in your casebook are from many jurisdictions

Casebooks contain cases from various state and federal courts. So the first case on battery may be from North Carolina and the next one from Florida. Even if all the elements of battery are the same, the way those components have evolved in each state through the years may mean that very different standards are used. The North Carolina case may represent the more common interpretation of the rule (the majority rule) and the Florida case may represent a less common, but not unique, interpretation (minority rule).

You may find yourself confused. You thought you understood the North Carolina case, but now you read the Florida case and it doesn't make sense in light of what you thought you knew. At this point you might reread both cases thinking you must have missed something. Or worse, you might think you are not cut out for law school. Neither is necessarily true. Unless you have an unusually sympathetic casebook editor, who deigns to include an explanatory note, you are unlikely to realize that one opinion represents the majority rule and the other applies the minority rule.

2. Casebook editors often try to "hide the ball"

Casebooks, especially those for first-year students, could be more useful if the editors remembered that you are a novice and that they have voluntarily taken on the task of helping you to become an expert. Sometimes the casebook editor has included cases for a reason that has nothing to do with the topic of the chapter. Some casebook editors like to put poorly decided cases adjacent to well-decided ones. This can drive you crazy. You are new to the law. Even if you thought one didn't make sense, who are you as a first-year student to know better than a sitting judge or an experienced law school professor? If a case makes no sense to you, you cannot use it for any purpose. It cannot teach you a legal rule nor can it help you learn how to analyze legal argument.

A colleague of one of the authors told the following story about his first few years of teaching. Because he was new to teaching, he adopted one of the popular casebooks. During the summer before his first class, he found that he had to call the authors of the casebook three times because, even with the teachers' manual, he didn't understand what they had done. In an exasperated voice he said, "They included the major rule of law in a footnote. The principal case in the section was one they included because it was poorly decided." Since he is not a "hide the ball" type, two years later he began work on his own book, a problem-oriented book with only ten cases.

Most casebook editors truly believe that they are contributing greatly to your education by giving you challenging material. However, many of them have difficulty thinking back to the time when they knew nothing about the law. The professors at your school who truly want to help you learn are caught in a bind. For the most part, unless they develop their own materials (a time-consuming process) they must use one of the traditional casebooks. If you are fortunate, your professor has selected one of the casebooks that is more student-accessible. But even so, you will need guidance to fully understand what the casebook authors had in mind.

The Ultimate Goal

Before we discuss case briefing and outlining—two important tools—we need to first talk about the ultimate goal of your first-year torts course. In other words, to understand the specific tools you will be using, you first need to know **what** it is you will be trying to do. That will help you understand **how** and **why** these tools should be used.

On a day-to-day basis, most of your professors will assign some pages in the casebook, and expect you to read the cases and understand them to the best of your ability. In class, discussion will center on the cases. The professor will ask questions about what was decided, why the case was decided the way it was, and then will likely push the class to consider whether the court was correct in its analysis. But in most instances this is not what you will be expected to do on the final exam. On the final exam, you will be expected to know what the rules are for various torts (including majority and minority rules). You will be given a fact pattern, and your job will be to identify what possible torts occurred, and then, applying the rules, discuss whether or not a successful cause of action can be made out for each of those possible torts. In other words, while the day-to-day class discussion is likely to focus on identifying exactly what rule the court used in its decision, and then critiquing whether that is or is not a good rule and whether the case was correctly decided, the final exam will ask you to APPLY new facts to the existing rules. We will say more about the final exam shortly, but as we discuss briefing and outlining, keep in mind what we have already said.

Taking Notes on Cases—Briefs?

Obviously one reason to brief cases is to be able to discuss that particular case in class (or to follow the discussion when the professor is calling on other students). Depending on your professor, you may be more or less inclined to brief every case. But if we assume that another key reason to read cases in law school is to learn how to take the facts of a client's problem and apply them to the law in such a manner that your client wins, then the important pieces of information you should get from each case come into sharper focus. These are the things you want to get out of a case you read:

1. The legal theory of recovery (the cause of action—e.g. battery, false imprisonment, negligence);
2. The element of the legal theory at issue in the case;

3. The element or elements at issue;
4. the facts of the reported case (insofar as they are relevant to the legal theory);
5. the court's decision as to whether the elements of the rule are satisfied; and
6. The reasons given for the court's decision (so that you can later use similar arguments). This may merely involve a rather mechanical application of the facts to the elements of the legal theory of the case, but often will include other factors that might have pushed the court in one direction or another in a close case.

The first thing you may notice is that the order we are suggesting for the components of your brief is probably different from the one you were given by your legal writing professor, or the one you saw in an assigned book in your legal writing class or elsewhere. Why is this so? Remember what we said about the ultimate goal—applying new facts to the rules of law established by the courts over time? The format we are suggesting for briefing puts that goal front and center. We suggest you identify the governing rule (and its elements) FIRST, so that you get practice starting your analysis from the rules and elements. This will reinforce the process of stating what the governing rule is first, and then applying the new facts to that rule or rules.

There is another reason for our suggested format. If you are presented with a new set of facts, or if you are an attorney with a client sitting in front of you telling you their story, how do you know which of the myriad facts are relevant? You will, with practice, know which facts are relevant because the existing rules tell you what to look for. If it's an actual client, once you have figured out the ballpark you're playing in (this looks like an intentional tort and not a breach of contract), you would then think about the governing rules and elements. For example, if it looks like a possible battery, one of the elements is a "contact." So you would ask your client, "Did the defendant ever touch you, or make contact with you in any way, directly or indirectly?" If the answer is YES, that element is satisfied, and you would then think about and try to apply the other elements. If the answer is NO, then one of the elements of battery is missing, so you would know that this cannot be a battery, and you would try to think of other torts it might be (for example, an assault, infliction of emotional distress, or negligence).

The **same approach** applies to a fact pattern presented to you by your professor—on an exam or in class. But instead of asking the live client, you are questioning the fact pattern. The rules and elements tell you what you need **from** that fact pattern to satisfy a particular element. The mother of one of the authors would ask him, when he was home from law school on vacation and was looking in the kitchen for something to eat, "What are you looking for?" He would answer, "I don't know." And she would respond, "Well, then how will you know when you've found it?" Wise words. You can't begin to analyze a legal problem until you know what you are looking for. The existing rules (broken down into elements wherever possible), will tell you what you are looking for. You will learn those rules from reading the cases, from class discussion, or from reading outside sources. You will then, in a fact pattern-based exam question, be expected to examine the facts presented to see if those elements are satisfied or not. At its core, and in its simplest form, this is what "legal analysis" is about. And this is what you are likely to be asked to do at the end of the course, on your final exam. During the semester the professor may want you to "state the case" in class. If so, your preparation will have to include that. But zeroing in on the issues presented, the rules that govern, and applying facts to those rules, is the ultimate goal.

Although we have said that what you are doing as a student is related to what lawyers do, there are some differences in emphasis. As a practicing lawyer, you would need to take much more from a case. You would need to know which court decided the case to determine its precedential value (was it a court in your state? Was it the highest court?). You would also need to understand the procedural posture of the case in greater detail so you could tell how important the facts were to the decision. Obviously if you have a professor who emphasizes the procedural posture of cases, you should pay attention to that section. If your professor does not emphasize procedural issues, at a minimum you should pay attention to a more basic question (as mentioned before)—sometimes the appellate court opinion you are reading tells you who wins the case. But sometimes the appellate court merely announces that one party (in torts, almost always the plaintiff) has a **chance** of winning the case, assuming they can prove certain things when the case goes back to the lower court. In other words, the appellate court has told the lower court what the governing rule is (what must be demonstrated), but not whether the plaintiff has in fact demonstrated it.

Almost all law schools teach their first-year students how to "brief." This is a bit strange because the information in most traditional brief formats is the information useful to the practicing lawyer, not to the law student. What is even stranger is that professors ask you for this information in class. We believe that they ask you all this detail because they want you to focus on the importance of the decided cases and the reasoning the judge used in writing the opinion. These are worthwhile goals. But the effect this has on students is often very negative.

Cases and Classes

This emphasis on cases as a teaching technique is a major cause of student exhaustion and confusion. You spend far too much time reading cases and writing "briefs" and far too little time thinking. When students are asked what the point of the case is, they often can't say. However, they *can* say that the defendant's car was blue. When students look at their professors' exams and the student answers that received A's, they are astonished and depressed to find that none of the detail they are spending hours prepping is relevant to the final exam. Yet they do not change their approach. Why? They say it is because they are afraid of being called on in class and not knowing the detail. So let's focus on two distinct issues here. First, let's focus on what happens in class.

Public humiliation is not fun. To avoid it some students spend countless hours on each and every case assigned. Others take a different approach. They buy books that "brief" the major cases for them. If you have heard a fellow student give what you thought was a brilliant response to a professor's question about a case in class, don't be surprised if that brilliant response came from a book of canned briefs, not from that student's head. The reality of law school is that almost everyone is confused—probably including that student who impressed you so much in class.

Perhaps there is a middle ground between endless hours that will not pay off and the shortcut of canned briefs. You can continue to benefit from what is good about the law school experience without becoming discouraged. One important starting point is to decide how to handle the problem of being called on in class. There are probably many solutions, but here are two you might consider.

The first is to take the approach that since almost everyone in your class is confused, if you can't answer the professor's questions if you are called on, no one will think you are stupid. Everyone else will just be glad he or she is not taking the heat. Add to this the knowledge that not having all the answers in class will have little or no effect on your grade. If you have read and thought about the case at all, you will be able to say enough for the professor to realize you have done your work. Most schools that give any points at all for class participation give only a few, and almost all professors who do announce it in advance. If you start using your time to formulate an organized approach to analyzing legal problems instead of taking the time to write detailed notes about every case, the points you will gain on your exam will far exceed the few you might lose in class participation.

Another approach is to take notes only on the analytically important aspects of your cases. When you read the case, highlight the kinds of detail your professor might ask about in a different color. You will be ready for class, but you will not have pages and pages of notes that are irrelevant the day after the case is discussed in class because they aren't focused on the kind of analysis you will be expected to do on the final.

Note Taking—Keeping the Goal in Mind

So, now we've taken care of prepping for **class**. The second issue—the more important one—is what kind of notes you should be taking to perform well when it matters—on the final exam. We will give you some preliminary advice here; there will be more as the discussion of legal analysis, outlining, and exam taking unfolds in the rest of the book.

Some students find it helpful to take notes on cases only after they have read a whole section of cases on one topic. They can't understand the first case in a section until all the cases are on the table, and some context is clear. If you want to take this approach, you will probably read all the cases through quickly the first time you encounter them, without taking any notes. Then you will go back to the beginning of the section later, read each case again and take notes. The quick overview of the cases can save you a great deal of time. Often in this quick reading you can identify the cases which were included to provide a historical background but which did not require detailed note taking. You can also identify cases which were included to provide a good example of the rules in this area of law or their application and therefore *did* require detailed note taking.

One thing many students say after their first year of law school is that they wish they had read some material about the subject matter of the section before they read the cases. We all learn best when we have a context for our learning. The technique of reading the whole section of cases quickly at the beginning may work, or a more detailed first reading may make sense. But either way, reading some context material can help you get more out of each case the first time around. Look for something short in your law school bookstore that fits your style of learning. One of the things that students ask professors all the time is, "What is the best commercial outline or hornbook for the class?" You have to keep this in mind—there is no one outside source that is best for every student. And there is also no one outside source that is best for every task. For **this** task—getting an overview to put the material in context—you want something short and sweet. Details of particular rules are not important for this purpose. In fact, too many rules will only confuse you if you try to read context material before each section of case material, and will take too much time. Books such as those in the *Mastering Series* published by Carolina Academic Press may be helpful to you for this purpose.

More About What Happens in Class

There is more we can say about the issue of preparing for class. One bit of advice is—don't obsess! If you don't understand what a case is about, just write down a few facts and what you think the governing rules are so that you will recognize the case when it is discussed. You will find out soon enough—in the next class—what is important.

Speaking of what happens in class (and how it relates to your reading), another piece of advice may make following the class discussion easier. It may also reduce your anxiety in the event that your professor uses random calling and zeroes in on you. In a classroom discussion (and when you are reading any case material), you should be aware of what the professor is trying to get you to learn. There are at least three major tasks that the professor may be trying to get a student in class to engage in:

1. identifying the rule—pulling the "holding" out of the court's opinion and stating it clearly;
2. debating whether the rule the court has decided to follow is a good one—are there policy arguments that support this rule or that argue for rejecting it (and might argue for an alternative rule); and
3. applying the facts of the case (or a new set of facts) to the rule—taking the rule as settled as a given (even if it may not be a good rule, and even if it may not be crystal-clear).

As we have said before, many professors spend most of class time on tasks one and two, even if the final exam will be primarily or exclusively about doing task number three. And in class, it is often confusing to students who think the discussion is about task number one, when the professor has moved on to task number two. Always try to be clear in your own mind about which is being discussed.

No book can tell you how to take notes on cases in order to be prepared for the exact approach to class discussion taken by your professors; they will each be different. Some professors will mention all of the following components of a case in class; other professors may never refer to them specifically. However, all of these will be helpful for you to know for exam preparation purposes. The basic format for taking notes on cases includes:

1. the legal rule which governs the decision in the case;
2. the elements of that legal rule;
3. the element or elements at issue;
4. the relevant facts of the case (in light of the legal rule);
5. the application by the court of the facts to the rule (were the elements satisfied or not? In other words, the decision of the court); and
6. the reasoning behind the court's decision.

This format contains the crucial information from each case. You will find an example of this format in this book's section on battery.

Outlining—Perfection Not Needed

In order to analyze problems on an exam, you need to think about what a good exam answer requires. You will be presented with new fact patterns, and you will need to discuss what tort or torts have been committed. To do that, you will need to know what the rule is for each tort, preferably broken down into specific elements, sub-elements, elaborations, limitations, or any gloss the courts have put on interpretation, common grey areas, misapplications, and disputes, and any factors that might influence the court to find the element met or not met. In other words, everything you have learned about that tort.

What about the cases themselves? Remember what we've already said about cases—knowing them and discussing them carries the day-to-day class sessions, but is less important for the final exam. Unless your professor indicates otherwise, they should not be your primary focus.

But cases can serve two important purposes in your outline. The first is to act as a prompt—to remind you where you first learned of a particular rule, element, sub-element, etc. So it can be useful to put case names, and maybe a few sentences about the case, in your outline next to the rule or element that came from that case. But remember—most professors won't require you to cite the case as the source of the rule or element. They'll want you to know the rule with all its nuances. So using the case names in your outline is mainly a reminder to you—a prompt—and not something to necessarily memorize.

The second use of the cases is as illustrations of the application of a rule. So in your outline you will list a particular element of a rule, and then note that in one of the cases from the book, the court found that the element was satisfied given the facts of that case. Now you have in your outline an example of how that element is met or demonstrated. And you can now use the example from the case as you write your exam answer to argue that the facts given in the question are a stronger or weaker example of how that element is demonstrated. So you would write, "In the XYZ case, the court found there was an offensive contact (one of the elements of battery) when the defendant caused the plaintiff to slip and fall in front of the defendant." Here (in the facts of the exam question), where the defendant caused the plaintiff to slip and fall in front of the entire class, there is an even stronger argument that a reasonable person would find that offensive. In other words, you can use the decided cases you studied to argue by analogy: "if the court found the rule met in that case, these facts are even stronger." Or conversely, "the court found the rule was met in that case, but here the facts are not as strong, so this might not meet the test." For most professors, you can write a good answer and get a good grade without ever using a case name. But using cases as the basis for analogies will often gain you additional points beyond those available for identifying the element and then discussing the basic application of the new facts to it.

There are almost as many ways to construct an outline as there are law students. But the guiding principle has to be this—working back from what a good answer will look like, what information would you need to have in your mind at the time of the exam to write that good answer? In other words, knowing what the final exam will require of you, you can **reverse engineer** what needs to be in your outline. You know you will need the rules, and the elements of those rules. But it will also be helpful to have in your mind the subelements, elaborations, limitations, or any gloss the courts have put on interpretation, common grey areas, misapplications, and disputes, and any factors that might influence the court to find the element met or not met.

Since that is what you want to have available to you in your mind while writing the exam based on a new fact pattern, that is what you should try to capture in your outline. That means you may want to try to write down everything and then, as you learn the material, keep shortening your outline until it is of manageable length. All well and good. But the process of creating the outline is only one part of the equation. Keep in mind that you don't want to spend so much time on your outline that there remains too little time to learn how to analyze exam questions and to practice that process of analysis.

Another approach is to try to develop a draft outline from your context reading. Then, instead of taking notes on each case individually, you can insert case material right into the outline. You will probably modify your outline as you go through the cases, but this technique focuses you on the structure of the area of the law you are studying right from the beginning. You can insert the information you get from class discussion of the cases into the outline after class. This means you never have to face the task most daunting to first-year students—figuring out how to take the raw material from class and turn it into the construction of the course outline; you will be constructing it right from the beginning. If you know yourself as one who obsesses over detail, this approach might be worth a try so you don't burn out before your first exam.

This book contains sample draft outlines for each topic that you can modify to fit your course. Most people associate the term "outline" with the traditional formal structure that is taught in high school (i.e., upper-case Roman numeral, followed by indented upper-case letter, then further indented Arabic numeral, then lower-case letter, etc.). Your law school outlines need not follow that format. They can be structured in any way that helps you organize, learn, recall, and apply the information they contain. If the traditonal format works best for you, by all means use it. If you find the formal outline style gets in your way, discard part or all of it. This book has sample outlines in both styles.

Components of an outline for each tort or defense

Elements

Sub-elements (of any given element)
- Elaborations and limitations
- Factors
- Common grey areas and disputes

Common counter-arguments (for any given element or sub-element)

Case examples
- To prompt memory of a rule
- To argue by analogy—(these facts are stronger/weaker than the XYZ case)

Policy ("black letter policy")
- **Arguments based on rights or fairness**
  - Compensation
  - Fault
  - Corrective justice
- **Arguments based on outcomes or utilitarianism**
  - Deterrence
  - Ability of plaintiff or defendant to insure
- **Arguments based on institutional considerations** (a type of utilitarian argument)
  - Proper role of courts vs. legislature in changing a particular rule

Remember the goal—include everything you know about the tort. Also keep in mind that an outline should be functional. It should be organized in the way arguments are likely to be presented. If there is a common counter-argument to a particular argument, that counter-argument should be in your outline right after the argument. For example, for an assault it is often said that "mere words" are not enough. But the exception would be when the words themselves convey a serious and immediate threat. So in your outline, in the proper place (we'll show you a sample in the next chapter) under the element "Act," your outline might then say "mere words are not enough." And then it would have the exception or counter-argument to that normal rule.

Law School Testing—A Shock

"Trace the development of the doctrine of strict liability."

"What were the facts most important to the court's decision in *Palsgraf*?"

"Discuss the relationship between the growth of the railroads and the law of negligence."

Although essay and "think" questions like those above *may* appear on your first-year torts exam, you probably will see no more than one. This may be a surprise to you. These questions (especially the first example above) are similar in style to the history or political science exam questions you probably encountered in undergraduate school ("discuss the five causes of the French Revolution"). Moreover, you may have been led to expect questions like these because they seem to reflect what your professor focuses on in class—development of the law, critique of particular cases or doctrines, policy, and historical context.

You may have professors who focus in class entirely on individual cases, requiring you to be prepared to recite in detail the facts of these cases. They may spend no time connecting the cases to one another or to the general principles underlying the law of torts. If your professor teaches in this way, you might expect your exam to consist of questions like the *Palsgraf* question above. On the other hand, you may have professors who spend class time reflecting on and debating about how different experts view the purposes of the law of torts. Logically, you would expect questions like the third example we've suggested. Unfortunately, few professors make it clear that the structure and content of their class sessions provide little guide to the structure and content of their final exams.

Although many professors include one "think question" on the final exam, most law school torts questions are stories ("issue spotter" fact patterns) that are carefully constructed to test a student's ability to recognize and analyze the legal theories suggested by the facts presented in these stories. Professors assume that the students who can competently analyze these usually fictitious stories will be able to competently analyze the legal issues presented in the stories told to them by their future clients. This may be true. But if you haven't figured out the likely format of the final exam, you will not have a real chance to demonstrate this skill.

You probably know that law students hardly wax enthusiastic about issue spotter exams. However, they may be a valid way for law schools to prepare you for the realities of practice. If professors had the inclination, and could handle the logistical problems, they might prefer to have all students role-play an interview with a client to demonstrate their mastery of the legal theories they have been studying (or draft a document, or engage in other demonstrations of "lawyering skills"). While there is a trend in this direction, most first-year courses will have little or none of this, and if they do, it is unlikely to be the dominant method of assigning the final grade.

One could imagine the following scenario as the basis for an exam question:

> Attorney Oliver James was sitting in his office when he got a phone call from a Phillip North. Mr. North was obviously agitated.
>
> "My son Bill is in the hospital. The doctors told us that he'll eventually be OK, but it will be a long while. He was riding his tricycle in our driveway when Jane, the girl next door, came home from school. She knocked him down off the tricycle and kicked him. We heard him crying and went outside. We have insurance that will cover the medical bills. But we think that little bully should be stopped. Is there anything we can do?"
>
> "Mr. North, you mentioned that your son was on a tricycle. How old is he?"
>
> "Only five."
>
> "And how old is Jane?"
>
> "Six."
>
> [Mr. James thought, "There might be a claim for battery. There is clearly a harmful contact. I don't think children under seven are excluded from liability in this state, but I'll have to check that out. If not, I have to make sure that we can prove that Jane was capable of forming the intent. Mr. North did call her 'bully.' I need more information."]
>
> "Mr. North, tell me about Jane."
>
> "She's only one of a whole family of uncontrollable children. She has three older brothers who are the terrors of the neighborhood and have trained her well. Of course, I suppose the parents should be blamed. They don't make any effort to make them behave."

[Mr. James thought, "It sounds as if we may have a claim against both child and parents. It seems as if Jane is capable of having formed the intent to hurt Pete."]

Mr. James said, "So you're sure that Jane and Pete weren't playing a game, and Jane acted that way she did because she was too young to know the consequences."

"Oh yes," replied Mr. North emphatically. "I'm sure Jane knew exactly what she was doing. I've talked to several neighbors since yesterday, and they all have the same impression of Jane. They have complained to the parents about all the children. In the case of my son, he had just received the tricycle for his birthday. He was out having fun by himself.

Mr. James said, "Mr. North, I'm quite sure that you have a case, but I need to check on one detail. If you don't hear from me before then, please come in on Monday at 3 p.m. to discuss the matter."

For better or worse, demonstrating knowledge in law school must be done in a format that allows a whole class of students to show what they know and to perform at the same time. The James/North conversation becomes the following short issue-spotting fact pattern:

Five-year-old Bill was in the driveway of his parents' house riding his tricycle when Jane came home from school. She was the six-year-old youngest child of the next-door neighbors. Her three older brothers had a great influence on her, and all four children had a reputation in the neighborhood for being aggressive. Although the parents knew of their children's behavior, they did nothing to control them. Bill was at the end of the driveway when Jane arrived. She knocked him off the tricycle and kicked him. Is Jane liable to Bill for battery?

Again, note the similarity between what the real-life lawyer does and what you—the first-year student—are being asked to do. Of course the version presented to you on a written exam is shorter and more "simple" in the sense of being pared down. Also note that because you are NOT playing the role in front of the professor in his or her office, there is no opportunity for the professor to stop and ask you to clarify your answer. When you are **writing** an exam answer, you have **one chance** to demonstrate—as clearly as you can—everything you know about the law **as it relates to the problem presented to you.**

Grading—More Mystery

Law students come from all sorts of educational backgrounds. Some have been math or science majors, where arriving at the exact and precise right answer on an exam was very important. They may have had few courses in which much writing was required, and the timed writing of a law school issue spotter exam is daunting. Others have been literature, philosophy, or history majors. In those subjects they may have done little else but write. They were usually able to select the topic for their papers, and they were not restricted in how much time they spent, nor in the conclusion they reached. No undergraduate student (or graduate student, for that matter) is really prepared for the law school issue spotter exam.

Even after you understand the format of the issue spotter question, you may not clearly understand how faculty will grade your answers. Law students learn that they cannot trust their instincts about their performance. One semester you find that you enjoy one class more than any of the others. You spend a great deal of time working on it, and you walk into the final exam feeling very confident. You may have paid much less attention to your other courses, and you walk into those exams feeling unprepared. You should not be surprised if you get the same grade in all your courses or even get a lower grade in your favorite course. And to make it worse, the answer to an issue spotter is open-ended in the sense that you, the student, must generate the structure and decide what to say and how much. While taking the exam, you have no idea whether there is only one tort in the problem or more, and you therefore have no idea how well you have done. Unlike the French Revolution question mentioned earlier—where as you walk out of the exam room you at least know how many of the five causes you addressed—when you walk out of your law school exams, you will have a high level of uncertainty as to how well you did. For one thing, you may not even know which issues you were supposed to find. And for another, you won't really know how much detail each issue required.

Another potential problem is that you carry exam expectations with you from your past. If you were a math or science major, you may have spotted the issues in the fact pattern, but you may have come to quick conclusions about them (what is the "right" answer) without doing an analysis of the arguments on both sides. If you were a humanities major, you may have spotted the issues in the fact pattern, but you may have spent too much time in worrying about the style of your writing to have enough time to cover them all.

If you knew what your professor was looking for, obviously you would be able to adjust your exam writing style. However, many professors do not give you much guidance, at least not without being asked, and many seem to use different approaches to grading. Some professors have intricate, detailed score sheets for every exam question. Every time a student uses one of the words or concepts on that score sheet, that student gets a point. Depending on the professor, such a score sheet could have literally one hundred or more possible points for an exam. This is not the norm. Few faculty members have the stamina for that kind of grading. At the other extreme is the professor who reads each exam and, using what might charitably be called a "holistic" method, decides what grade the student deserves.

Most professors have some kind of score sheet, but they may use their score sheets in very different ways. This may have a profound effect on your grade. Some give you points for mentioning an issue even if you mention it in a way that is illogical. Some may award points for unconnected sentences scribbled as the last lines of an answer just before the end of the exam. Other professors give no points unless the issues are discussed in an organized fashion. Some professors give most of their points for philosophical or policy analysis, some give few.

Usually students who receive low grades are encouraged to talk to their professors about their performance to see if they have a problem with exam taking that could plague them for the rest of their law school careers. However, students often say that they leave their meetings with the professors more confused than ever because the professors are unable to explain why their answers are any different from ones that received A's. The difficulty may be that the discussion is taking place several months after the exam, and the professor may not remember what factors determined the grades. Many students are told that they "didn't apply the law to the facts." But the professor can't seem to explain how to do that.

This book is designed to train you to be skilled at *applying the facts to the law*. The best way to explain this process is to begin by assuming that all professors use some kind of score sheet to grade your exams so that they have a method of testing your ability to evaluate the words included in their questions as they relate to each of the legal issues presented. The section on the tort of battery will provide an example of such a score sheet.

Exam Answers—Need for Practice

There are two components to a successful exam answer. The first is knowledge of the law. This is what your casebook is intended to give you (though perhaps in a less straightforward manner than you might desire). The second is conducting legal analysis and presenting that analysis in writing your answer. Casebooks do not prepare you to do this analysis. They are organized by cause of action/legal theory, and then sometimes (but not always) by elements of that legal theory. For example, you will read all the cases about the tort of battery in one section of the book. You will also read all the cases about each element of battery in a separate subsection. By the time you have reached the end of the chapter on battery, you may have learned the common interpretations of each of the elements. However, you will have had no practice in applying your knowledge to a lawyer/client situation. Therefore, you will have had no practice in doing what you will be asked to do on your final exam—to demonstrate that you know the law of intentional torts as it relates to a new situation (the fact pattern you will be presented).

Make no mistake about it—learning the legal rules is hard. But the harder of the two components is the analysis and writing. It is quite difficult to write a coherent answer. Most students, if the professor stopped them on the way into the exam, could rattle off the elements of each tort. Yet years of experience tells us that most students will not properly use those elements to frame their own sentences and string them together into coherent paragraphs. Students assume that knowing the cases and the law is enough. They don't realize that doing legal analysis, and putting it in writing, is hard work.

It is very easy in class to convince yourself that you could give a coherent answer to the question the professor just asked (when you aren't the one called on). And it is also easy to convince yourself that, having learned and memorized the rules, you could easily and readily apply a new set of facts to them. But rest assured—from our experience we can tell you that even if students are given a packet of materials that includes a question, a list of the elements of the legal theory that is suggested by the fact pattern (including the words from the fact pattern that were included to relate to the elements), and an answer, and then the students are asked to write out their own answer, in many cases they won't be able to do it well. If you have done practice problems in class, or in your study group, or on your own, maybe you'll believe us. If not, please—take our word for it. Even with a sample answer in front of them, students have trouble framing their own sentences and stringing them together into coherent paragraphs. Don't assume that knowing the law is enough. Writing about it in a coherent way is difficult. That is why this book will suggest to you ways of organizing material that will help you get your thoughts down on paper efficiently. We can't guarantee it will be easy—our goal is to make it as easy as possible.

If analyzing exam questions and writing answers is difficult when there is only one legal theory to contend with, imagine the problems you will encounter on a typical law school exam. Your professors will expect you to know how several legal theories relate to each other and sometimes compete with each other, but they will also expect you to know how to write logical answers to their questions.

"I panicked."

"I saw the issues, but I couldn't figure out how to talk about them."

"I got lost in the middle of my answer and never finished."

"I talked about battery, but I never got to anything else."

"I had no idea how to organize the answer."

These are the comments we hear from students every year. They always say, "I knew the stuff cold." They may actually be right, because they mean that they learned the material as it was presented in the casebook and discussed in class. They thought it was enough to learn their outlines, and they worked exceptionally long hours in learning them. However, they were doomed from the start because they had not learned to organize the outline in a usable way and then to demonstrate what they knew.

Since you must show your professors that you can relate the new facts in the issue spotter to the law, it is helpful to know and understand an answer format you can turn to under the stress of an exam. The analysis of each cause of action or legal theory should start with the rule for the theory that will be discussed. The rule should be presented as a series of elements (and sub-elements) if at all possible. Then you should go in a step-by-step manner to show why each element is or is not met. In some cases this will mean merely citing a few words from the fact pattern to show that the element is clearly met. In other cases, it may require many sentences discussing why the element might be met, and then setting out the arguments as to why the element is not met. After arguing both sides of the issue for any contested element, you should come to a conclusion (which often will not be definitive) and move on to the next legal theory. Sometimes the conclusion might be unambiguous ("all elements are met, therefore the cause of action will be successful"), but usually you will have to hedge a bit ("if the court interprets the first element broadly, it is met, and if so, then the other elements are easily met and so the cause of action will be successful").

As you write your answer, always keep in mind the main objective of the issue spotting exam—you are trying to show the professor that you clearly know what the law is **and** how the new facts presented to you on the exam apply to the law. So, as a general rule, every sentence you write should tell the professor either:

- something that needs to be demonstrated ("the first element the plaintiff must demonstrate is the intent to commit a battery") or
- that the facts of this case demonstrate or do not demonstrate that the element is met ("here, the defendant admitted that she wanted to hit the plaintiff and injure him, so the first element is met").

Of course what needs to be demonstrated might not be a one- or two-word element, but may include more subtle definition, or involve other sub-elements. And the facts may not absolutely fit the element, in which case you will argue how closely they do or don't fit. But the key is to always keep in mind your objective, and then to proceed, step by step, through each legal theory that is arguably raised by the fact pattern. Each chapter in this book will provide you with analysis hints and sample questions so that you can practice your writing.

Practicing the Method

There's an old joke about Carnegie Hall that we can adapt to fit law school:

> First-year student asks third-year student— "How do I get to the law review office?"
>
> Third-year student's response— "Practice, practice, practice."

Practice is the key to your success on law school exams. It is not enough to listen to other students being quizzed in class about the cases. And do not be tempted to think it is enough to read the questions and answers in this book. Although this might help your understanding of the law, it will not prepare you for demonstrating everything you know about torts in a three or four hour exam. You will need to spend time working through answers and at least sometimes writing them out. The time spent writing out answers in your own words is time well spent. So where do you get the questions? Some professors may give you review problems to work on in or out of class. A few casebooks have such problems, and a few professors provide review problems of their own in class. But that means—at best—only occasional practice. An additional source of practice problems would be commercially published books that include problems.

There is another source of practice problems right there in front of you, but not quite obvious. It is your casebook. "But wait," you're thinking, "my book doesn't have review problems." Yes, but for any given topic, your casebook usually will have more than one case. The first case may lay out a general rule, with a second case or note cases adding something new to your knowledge—an additional sub-rule, a modification of the rule, or maybe an example of the rule's application. Once you have learned the basic elements (often in the first case) you can then use the next case as a practice problem, going through **all** the steps of analysis (not just using that second case for the additional sub-rule it adds).

Chapter 2

Intentional Torts

Your casebook's coverage of intentional torts may start with a discussion devoted to the general idea of intent, which of course is an element of all intentional torts. This can be confusing because one case may be about battery and the next one about assault. Without knowing the differences between these individual torts yet, you may be unable to fully understand the cases. And, as you will soon learn, the test for intent will be different for each intentional tort. You might find it helpful to ignore the specific information about each tort and concentrate on what the case says about intent. The cases may show you how the requirements for intent have changed over the years. Or they may show how precisely a plaintiff can demonstrate the requisite intent. For example, intent is most clearly demonstrated if the plaintiff can prove the defendant's conscious desire to harm—in other words, what was the defendant's subjective *purpose*? But intent can also be demonstrated by using substantial certainty—*inferring* the result the defendant desired based on the likelihood that the result would occur, even if the defendant will not admit that he desired the result. At some point you may also find it helpful to read a summary of the other elements of intentional torts elsewhere.

Intentional torts are not analytically the most difficult part of the course; all are element-based. Liability arises only if all elements of the tort are demonstrated by the plaintiff, and the defendant cannot successfully assert any defenses or privileges. The order in which you discuss the elements is probably not important to your professor; all that is necessary is that you discuss each one. But in order to develop a systematic method for approaching intentional tort questions, you will probably want to learn the elements of each tort in a certain order, and to use that order every time you address a problem with one or more intentional torts. Most professors write exam questions in which only one or two of the elements are at issue for a given tort. For the elements that are not at issue, you will probably just state the element (to show the professor that you know it) and then briefly refer to the words from the fact pattern that show that the element is satisfied. For example, one of the elements of battery is "contact." If the professor wishes to make it clear that contact is not to be discussed at length, she might use the word "touched" in the fact pattern. When elements are problematic, the wording will be less direct. There will be words to suggest the element is not satisfied, words to suggest it is. *Or*, and this is very important, the fact pattern may not give any facts at all relevant to that element, which means you must notice that a particular element is at issue without any facts to prompt your analysis. (This is one reason why we suggest the top-down approach below—in the section on test taking and grading.) You should discuss both sides of the issue—either how the element is or is not satisfied—using words from the fact pattern to support your argument. Your professor may want you to come to a conclusion, or the professor may just want you to show that you understand that one side of the argument may be stronger or weaker. Because the analytical approach for all intentional torts is similar, this book will cover only five intentional torts. You can apply the same analysis and writing techniques to any other intentional tort you study.

Lack of time is often a major problem in intentional torts questions. Most of them have several people doing nasty things to several other people. The trick is to make sure you find all the torts and cover them appropriately within the time allotted. Another problem for intentional torts questions is whether to organize your answer by tort or by party. Sometimes one method works better than the other. You will have the opportunity to practice both methods later in the book.

Battery

Case Reading and Note Taking

Below is a case which has one element of battery at issue. Deciding to use this case presented us with a dilemma often faced by authors of casebooks. The judge makes all the right points to illustrate a legal theory, but a wrinkle in the case makes it a difficult one: the plaintiff sued the defendant only for negligence, not for battery. Why do you suppose the plaintiff's attorney would do that? Because the lawyer knew that the defendant's insurance company would not pay if the defendant was found to have committed an intentional tort. So even though the facts suggest that the defendant caused the harm intentionally—not negligently—the jury (probably wanting to compensate a sympathetic plaintiff) found for the plaintiff. The judge then overturned the verdict of the jury. The highest court in the state agreed to hear the plaintiff's appeal without having the plaintiff go through the first level of review ("We allowed the plaintiff's application for direct review."). The court's opinion affirms the decision of the trial judge that there is no case for the plaintiff under a negligence theory. The tort that the defendant committed is battery. Normally a plaintiff wants the court to find the elements of a battery are met. In this case, unfortunately for the plaintiff, finding that there is a battery means that there is no insurance money for the injured child.

Waters v. Blackshear

412 Mass. 589 (1992)

WILKINS, J. On June 6, 1987, the minor defendant placed a firecracker in the left sneaker of the unsuspecting minor plaintiff Maurice Waters and lit the firecracker. Maurice, who was then seven years old, sustained burn injuries. The defendant, also a minor, was somewhat older than Maurice.[1] The defendant had been lighting firecrackers for about ten minutes before the incident, not holding them but tossing them on the ground and watching them ignite, jump, and spin.

Maurice and his mother now seek recovery in this action solely on the theory that the minor defendant was negligent.[2] The judge instructed the jury, in terms that are not challenged on appeal, that the plaintiffs could recover only if the defendant's act was not intentional or purposeful and was negligent. The jury found for the plaintiffs, and judgment was entered accordingly. The trial judge then allowed the defendant's motion for judgment notwithstanding the verdict on the ground that the evidence showed intentional and not negligent conduct. We allowed the plaintiffs' application for direct appellate review and now affirm the judgment for the defendant.

We start with the established principle that intentional conduct cannot be negligent conduct and that negligent conduct cannot be intentional conduct. *Sabatinelli v. Butler*, 363 Mass. 565, 567 (1973). The only evidence of any conduct of the defendant on which liability could be based, on any theory, is that the defendant intentionally put a firecracker in one of Maurice's sneakers and lit the firecracker.

The defendant's conduct was a battery, an intentional tort. See Restatement (Second) of Torts § 13 (1965) ("An actor is subject to liability to another for battery if [a] he acts intending to cause a harmful or offensive contact with the person of the other or a third person, or

1. The evidence does not disclose the defendant's age. One can infer that he was one or two years older than Maurice.

2. We infer that the decision not to assert a battery claim was based on the terms of available insurance coverage.

an imminent apprehension of such a contact, and [b] a harmful contact with the person of the other directly or indirectly results"); 1 F.V. Harper, F. James, Jr., & O.S. Gray, Torts § 3.3, at 272–273 (2d ed. 1986) ("to constitute a battery, the actor must have intended to bring about a harmful or offensive contact or to put the other party in apprehension thereof. A result is intended if the act is done for the purpose of accomplishing the result or with knowledge that to a substantial certainty such a result will ensue" [footnote omitted]); W.L. Prosser & W.P. Keeton Torts, §9, at 41 (5th ed. 1984) ("The act [of the defendant] must cause, and must be intended to cause, an unpermitted contact").

The intentional placing of the firecracker in Maurice's sneaker and the intentional lighting of the firecracker brought about a harmful contact that the defendant intended. The defendant may not have intended to cause the injuries that Maurice sustained. The defendant may not have understood the seriousness of his conduct and all the harm that might result from it. These facts are not significant, however, in determining whether the defendant committed a battery. See *Horton v. Reaves,* 186 Colo. 149, 155 (1974) ("the extent of the resulting harm need not be intended, nor even foreseen"). The only permissible conclusion on the uncontroverted facts is that the defendant intended an unpermitted contact. If the defendant were an adult, we would have no hesitancy in ruling, as a matter of law, that lighting a firecracker in Maurice's sneaker was an act that was intended to cause a harmful (and also an offensive) contact with Maurice.

The fact of the defendant's minority does not change our view. On this record, the jury would not have been warranted in concluding that the minor defendant did not intend that the unpermitted contact with Maurice be harmful. See *Horton v. Reaves, supra* ("the infant must appreciate the offensiveness or wrongfulness of his act"). The defendant did not testify. There was no evidence to suggest that for some special reason the defendant did not know the contact with Maurice would be harmful. The defendant was not so young that a person of his age, experience, and intelligence would not have understood the harmful nature of that contact. See Prosser & Keeton, *supra* § 134, at 1071. Cf. *Mann v. Cook,* 346 Mass. 174, 178 (1963) (negligence action). If the jury believed, as they must have, that the defendant did what the uncontroverted testimony indicated he did, as a matter of law the defendant acted intending to cause a harmful contact with Maurice. In short, there was no room for the jury to believe the uncontroverted evidence and to conclude nevertheless that the contact with Maurice was not intentionally harmful but was merely negligent.

Judgment affirmed.

Notes on the Case

Rule: Liability for battery requires that the defendant had the

1. **Intent** (to make or cause)
2. **Contact** (that was)
3. **Harmful or Offensive**

In addition (and this is a separate step **after** making out the elements of the prima facie case)—

4. The defendant has no valid **Defense**

Elements: intent, contact, harmful or offensive (may not all be spelled out in any given case)

Element(s) at issue: intent

Facts: A child of about nine years of age had been lighting firecrackers for about ten minutes, "**not holding them**" but always tossing them on the ground to watch them ignite. He then placed a firecracker in the sneaker of the "**unsuspecting**" seven-year-old plaintiff who was burned when the defendant lit the firecracker.

Decision: intent is satisfied; the other elements are also

Reasoning: A "person of his age, experience, and intelligence" would appreciate the possible harm. He did not hold the firecrackers (which suggests he knew they were dangerous).

So we can show at least that he intended some contact with the other child, and we almost certainly can infer that he intended that contact to be harmful or offensive. It is not necessary that he desired the exact harm, only that he intended some harm or offense (or in some jurisdictions, merely the contact itself).

The rule set forth in our notes above is not the rule stated in this Massachusetts case. Law school exams are not tied to any particular jurisdiction. Although the elements may be similar from state to state, the exact wording of a rule may not always be. You will want to learn the elements as your professor presents them. If your professor doesn't give you precise language, try to draw the elements from a case you used in class, the notes in your casebook, or from outside context reading (a hornbook or commercial outline). You may be asked to use the rules from one of the various Restatements. The key is to be as precise as possible, and to break down rules presented in compound, run-on sentences into component parts.

There is no one absolutely correct way to state a given rule. In general, if there is a separate step or idea that is useful in your analysis and that becomes a source of contention in cases, you should learn it as a separate element or sub-element. In the notes above, the idea of causation is incorporated in the intent element. Some hornbooks and cases list it as a separate element, and it's OK to do so. (And, obviously, if your professor lists it as a separate element, you should do so as well.) Our notes on the case show the elements of battery as they are commonly stated in casebooks and hornbooks, because causation is almost never at issue in a battery. But as you will see, in *negligence* causation is critically important and actually is addressed in two separate steps of the analysis.

Your outline should have more than just one or two word "elements." You should try to capture everything you have learned that is relevant; everything you know about the tort—elements, sub-elements, elaborations, limitations, or any gloss the courts have put on interpretation, common grey areas, misapplications, and disputes, and any factors that might influence the court to find the element met or not met. You also will want to flesh out the rule and elements you identified in your context reading with the information from the cases you read. What follows is a draft outline of battery, with the information about *Waters v. Blackshear* in the proper place—at "intent."

Draft Outline

Rule: Liability for battery requires that the plaintiff demonstrate the defendant's

1. **Intent** (to make or cause)
2. **Contact** (that was)
3. **Harmful or Offensive**

In addition (and this is a separate step **after** making out the elements of the prima facie case)—

4. The defendant has no valid **Defense** or privilege

1. Intent

a. a volitional act (as opposed to a reflex or someone physically forcing or coercing the defendant to move his arm)

b. with a conscious desire or purpose to make contact (in a single-intent jurisdiction)

   or a conscious desire or purpose to make a contact that will harm or offend (in a dual intent jurisdiction)[1]

---

1. Some professors will spend a lot of time on this; others will gloss over it. The Restatement of Torts does not give a clear answer. For the rest of this section, we will—for simplicity's sake—discuss battery problems applying the dual intent rule.

or the conscious desire or purpose to cause the plaintiff to be apprehensive of a battery (this is the intent standard for assault; the Restatement of Torts allows the intent for battery and the intent for assault to be used interchangeably—this is one version of the more general idea of transferred intent)

The ability of a child to form the necessary intent is determined on a case-by-case basis—(this is the majority rule)

Children under seven can never form the necessary intent—(this is the rule in a minority of jurisdictions)

There are different ways to prove the defendant had the requisite intent

direct evidence—defendant's own admission, defendant telling another person he was going to try to hurt the plaintiff, etc. (seldom available)

"**substantial certainty**" **test**—if the defendant did something that would inevitably lead to a certain outcome, we can infer that the defendant desired that outcome

transferred intent—if the defendant had the requisite intent to commit one of the other trespassory intentional torts (assault, false imprisonment, trespass to land, and trespass to chattels) we can transfer that intent to satisfy the intent to commit the battery

Here, the child was igniting firecrackers, throwing them on the ground and watching them explode (not holding them) before he put one in another "unsuspecting" child's shoe. This shows, in the absence of any other evidence, that the child was acting volitionally. It also shows that the child knew that the firecracker was dangerous, and therefore we can infer that he intended that the contact harm or offend, or that he was substantially certain that it would, and therefore we can conclude that he intended the outcome.

2. Contact

Can be by the defendant touching the plaintiff, by some extension of the defendant touching the plaintiff (for example, a stick), or by something set in motion by the defendant touching the plaintiff (for example, a thrown ball).

Here, there was a contact when the firecracker was put in the plaintiff's shoe, and a second (and more important) contact when the firecracker exploded.

3. Harmful or Offensive

This element is met when the contact is either harmful OR offensive

a. Harmfulness is judged by an *external* standard—if there is some minimal injury to the plaintiff

b. Offensiveness is judged by an *objective* standard. This means we don't look to see whether **this** plaintiff was offended, but rather whether a reasonable person in the plaintiff's position would be offended, given the circumstances; this is to prevent hyper-sensitive plaintiffs from recovering from a defendant who had no way to know that their behavior would be considered offensive.

Additional rule or exception (to how we judge "offensiveness")—defendant may be liable if the defendant **knows** that this plaintiff would find the touching to be offensive, even if a reasonable person would not consider it offensive

Here, we don't know whether there was "harm" as the court would define it—there might have been enough of an injury to the skin or a sudden pain that would qualify. There almost certainly is "offense" in the context of this situation, but you would need to discuss it.

There is another rule that comes into play (not an element):

If the defendant intends the contact, the defendant is responsible for all harm that results; it is not necessary to intend the full extent of the resultant harm, just the contact itself. (*Waters v. Blackshear*).[2]

4. Defenses (not a complete list, but the most common ones):

a. self defense
b. defense of others
c. consent
   1. express consent
   2. implied consent
d. public necessity
e. private necessity
f. discipline

---

2. This is a general rule for all intentional torts—if you commit the intentional tort, you are usually liable for all consequences. Your professor might bring this rule up now, or may discuss it later in the chapter on intentional torts. Or your professor may consider it an additional sub-rule under intent—the rule being that it doesn't matter if the defendant did not INTEND this particular result if intent is otherwise demonstrated.

These elements make out the prima facie case for battery. The common law has established that these three elements need to be demonstrated to successfully claim a battery. So we set out those elements, as well as other things we know about each of the elements or about the tort, including any factors that might influence the court to find the element met or not met, and then looked at the facts to see if these elements were **demonstrated. All** of the elements had to be met. (But notice that for one of them, we could demonstrate **either** that the contact was harmful **or** that it was offensive).

IF all the elements of the prima facie case are satisfied, that is not the end of it—the plaintiff does not necessarily win. The defendant can then argue that even if the prima facie case for battery is made, the defendant had one or more valid defenses.

Most cases you read in your casebook will have only one contested or debatable element, sub-element, or defense. Therefore, each case will usually appear only once in your outline (as *Waters v. Blackshear* does). But keep in mind that your outline should not be organized around the cases; it should be organized around the elements and sub-elements. So what do we do with the cases covered in class? This is where we go back to something we said earlier. On a day-to-day basis, knowing and understanding the cases is vitally important for your class preparation. But when it comes to outlining the material to use on an exam, the cases have a less important role.

You will want to use the cases in your outline for two basic purposes: first, to trigger your recall of a particular rule or element, and second, as one example of how an element is met or not met, which can then be used to argue by analogy. For example, in *Leichtman v. WLW Jacor Communications, Inc.*, 634 N.E. 2d. 697 (Ohio 1994), the court found that blowing cigarette smoke in the plaintiff's face could be considered "contact." So in the hypothetical case you are analyzing, where (let's assume) the defendant squirted the plaintiff with a can of aerosol deodorant, you would argue—based on *Leichtman*—that there is at least as strong a case, if not stronger, that the "contact" element is met.

Unless your professor says otherwise, he or she will probably not expect you to cite the specific name of a case as authority for a given element or rule. Your professor will likely want you to know and to present the elements, and then be able to apply new facts to them, but will not expect you to "footnote" their source. However, some professors will want you to know specific sections of the Restatement of Torts. If so, of course you will want to include those sections in your notes. But even if your professor doesn't require you to use cases, they can be helpful to you in your outline for the purposes we have suggested.

Now are we finished? Not quite. After you have gone step by step through each element, and then considered each possible defense, you may still want to consider anything else that might cause a court to decide in one direction or another, particularly if it is a close case.

Test Taking and Grading

We can use the Bill and Jane fact pattern from the first chapter as an example of what you can expect in an exam.

> Five-year-old Bill was in the driveway of his parents' house riding his tricycle when Jane came home from school. She was six years old, and the youngest child of the next-door neighbors. Her three older brothers had a great influence on her, and all four children had a reputation in the neighborhood for being aggressive. Al-

> though the parents knew of their children's aggressive behavior, they did nothing to control them. Bill was at the end of the driveway when Jane arrived. She knocked him off the tricycle and kicked him. Is Jane liable?

If Jane had been an adult, there would be no uncertainty about battery. When you saw in the fact pattern that someone pushed someone else, you probably suspected that there might be a battery (and possibly other intentional torts). But the person who wrote this question made a point of telling you that Jane is only six years old. This was the clue that you needed to zero in on the part of your outline concerning the ability of young children to form the requisite intent. You probably read a case (maybe it was just a note case) about the age at which children are held to be capable of forming the requisite intent to be held liable for committing an intentional tort. Although Jane is only six, you are told that she and her brothers "had a reputation in the neighborhood for being aggressive." Therefore, your starting point might be to say that the majority rule is that whether a young child can have the requisite intent is decided on a case-by-case basis. So you have stated the rule, but now you need to apply it. So you would go on to say that there might be a presumption or a general inclination for a court to find that a six-year-old cannot have intent. But *here*, because the child has a reputation for being aggressive, a court might find that there *was* intent.

Is that all we know about this topic? No. We also know that in a minority of jurisdictions, a child under the age of seven *cannot* be found to have the requisite intent. *If* that rule applies in this jurisdiction, then a court *cannot* find this child liable. Do we know which rule applies to the exam question? Unless the exam told you which rule applied, a complete answer would argue in the alternative—if the court follows the majority rule, then maybe plaintiff can show intent, maybe not. If the court follows the minority rule, then the plaintiff cannot.

Notice what that complete answer looks like to the professor reading it. You have shown that you know the majority rule, and shown that you can apply these new facts to it (in this case, making an argument and a counter-argument). And you have also shown that you know the minority rule, and you have explained how the facts of this case would apply to that rule. Your notes for "intent" would contain both rules, and once you recalled them, you would discuss whether the element is met. Your notes for the other elements would set out what is required to meet each of them, and in this fact pattern, it would be fairly clear that they are met (but unless your professor indicated otherwise, you would want to list those other elements and quickly indicate how they are met).

Notes for Answer

Intent

Argument against:
six years old

Argument for:
"reputation in the neighborhood for being aggressive"

Contact—"knocked him off the tricycle and kicked him"

Harmful or offensive—"knocked him off the tricycle and kicked him"

Remember, your approach should be to identify a possible tort, and then to recall everything you know about that tort: elements, sub-elements, elaborations, limitations, or any gloss the courts have put on interpretation, common grey areas, misapplications, and disputes, and any factors that might influence the court to find the element met or not met. Or stated another way—everything that needs to be demonstrated by the plaintiff or that would be helpful to the plaintiff because it is legally relevant. Then you look at the facts and apply them to the elements and sub-elements, etc., to see if an element is satisfied, a grey area comes into play, etc. In other words, is each element or component demonstrated? Having gone through this, step by step, you have done your "top-down" analysis. But you are not finished! In order to ensure that you have not missed anything important, it is helpful to go back to the fact pattern and go fact by fact, crossing out or underlining the words you already have used in your quick notes for the answer. Unmarked words may require your attention or may just advance the story—you want to at least pause and think about whether any of the facts suggest something that you have not already addressed in your top-down analysis. This is doing analysis from the "bottom-up."

The more fact patterns you read, the better you become at determining which words have legal significance and which don't. But here is the key point—do the top-down analysis first. *Then*, to make sure you haven't missed anything, do the bottom-up analysis.

Why? One reason (the less important one) is demonstrated by our simple example above. Notice that a single fact may fit into more than one element. If you organize your answer based on the facts—labeling the legal significance of each fact as it goes by—you are likely to miss some points.

But there is a second and more important reason. Think about the dynamics of a final exam. It's the end of the semester; you have all this information swirling in your head (not only from your torts course, but for all of your exams). You are looking at a new set of facts in a time-pressured situation.

Now, you have two choices. You can organize your thinking around the fact pattern you were just presented with and have been reading for 15 *minutes*.

Or you can draw on everything you have learned about torts, going about your analysis in a step-by-step manner, organizing your answer based on material you've had 15 *weeks* to process. If you are like most students, using the top-down approach first, and organizing your answers around material you have spent the whole semester learning and refining, is going to be a better bet.

Following is the fact pattern with the words used in the Notes for Answer underlined.

> Five-year-old Bill was in the driveway of his parents' house riding his tricycle when Jane came home from school. She was six years old, and the youngest child of the next-door neighbors. Her three older brothers had a great influence on her, and all four children had a reputation in the neighborhood for being aggressive. Although the parents knew of their children's aggressive behavior, they did nothing to control them. Bill was at the end of the driveway when Jane arrived. She knocked him off the tricycle and kicked him. Is Jane liable?

If this were a thirty-minute question, the score sheet would look something like this:

Issue spotted — Battery (probably no points because it's a single-issue question)

Rule/Elements:

Intent	1
Volition	1
Apply facts—here, no contrary evidence/can assume it was volitional	1
To make a harmful/offensive contact (remember, we're using dual intent test)	1
Apply facts—here, no direct evidence of purpose	2
Substantial certainty	1
Apply facts—here, a child would appreciate the consequences	3
Can child of this age form intent?	1
Majority rule/ad hoc judgment about the child	1
Apply — here, for a child may be hard to find intent	3
Apply — counter: this child had reputation for being aggressive	3
Minority rule/can't form intent	2
Apply — here, that would mean the element isn't met	1
Contact	1
Apply—here, a given	1
Harmful or offensive	1
Apply—here, clearly harmful	1
Here, may be offensive (depending on context)	up to 3

You could get up to 21 points for your discussion of intent, if you do it perfectly. That's a lot of points, but just a little more effort—going through the other elements step by step—can earn you another 7 points, some of which are fairly easy points to earn.

It is important for every law student to realize that a trial lawyer must prove all elements of a cause of action. Your professor will want to see whether students can present each and every element that needs to be satisfied, and point to the words in the fact pattern that suggest that an element is satisfied. That is why the score sheet above contains so many points for the elements as well as the application of the facts to the elements. (Of course there would probably be as many different score sheets for this question as professors using the question.)

The answer format used in this book contains the following:

(a) the statement of the relevant legal theory (what tort or defense is arguable);

(b) the rule for that legal theory (or a clear statement of whether each element has to be met or whether the following list is merely a set of factors);

(c) the elements that must be demonstrated and then an application of the facts of the question to show that the element in question is demonstrated and why;

(d) as much discussion as is necessary of any of the elements that are contested, including sub-elements, common arguments pro and con, identification of gray areas in that element and how they come into play, arguments by analogy from cases already decided in comparison to these facts;

(e) identification of any applicable defenses and their elements, and discussion of whether those elements are satisfied or not; and

(f) a conclusion (which some professors want you to give and others may not want).

Answer

Bill may have a claim in battery.

Liability for battery requires:

1. intent
2. contact
3. which was harmful or offensive
4. with no applicable defenses

(1) The element at issue is intent. In a minority of jurisdictions children under seven are immune from tort liability because they are deemed to be unable to form the

requisite intent. In such a jurisdiction Jane would not be liable, as a matter of law, since she is only six. However, in a majority of jurisdictions a child's ability to form the necessary intent is determined on a case-by-case basis. Although it could be argued that Jane at six is too young to form the requisite intent to commit a battery (given the existence of the minority rule), the better argument is that she did have intent. She has "a reputation in the neighborhood for being aggressive." Her actions would allow a jury to infer that she intended to harm or offend Bill, even if she did not come out and say so.

(2) Jane kicking Bill constitutes a contact—her foot making direct contact with him. Her knocking him down also constitutes a contact—her hand making contact with him. And the resulting contact of Bill with the ground might constitute a third contact. Of course only one contact is required to satisfy this element.

(3) Being pushed or knocked down like this would almost certainly be considered offensive (as judged by the reasonable person). If there is any physical injury to Bill—a bruise, for example, or a skinned knee—then the contact is also harmful.[3]

(4) There do not appear to be any defenses.

Therefore, Jane is probably liable for battery.

Particularly at the early stages of your course, your professor is probably looking primarily for your knowledge of the rules and your ability to apply new facts to those rules. But you might want to include some policy arguments about the difficulties in deciding whether to hold young children responsible for intentional torts. In other words, in addition to stating the existing rule (in this case there is both a majority and minority rule), you may also want to indicate that you understand why there is a disagreement as to which rule—minority or majority—is better.

Remember what we talked about in Chapter One—this is different from discussing *whether* or not the elements of the rule are satisfied. Some jurisdictions (a minority) have solved the problem by establishing a bright line test—no child under seven can be found to have the required intent, and therefore no child under seven can be liable for an intentional tort. This makes the job of the court easier (in fact, if the rule is clear the case will never get to court in the first place). But it means that some people will be injured without having recourse, even though the child in question was actually able to form the tortuous intent. Of course, the younger the child, the more difficult it may be to get a clear picture of his capacity to form the intent. Do we really want to

3. Remember—this element merely requires that the contact be EITHER harmful OR offensive. But if it is both, you should say so, making clear that you know that only one or the other is necessary.

be questioning young children in court? Do we really believe that such a young child would clearly understand the questioning and be able to give an accurate answer? Because of those doubts, the law may reject what seems on its face to be a better rule—let's decide every child's capacity on a case-by-case basis—in favor of the bright line test, even if a few victims are thus barred from compensation. This tension—case-by-case decisions versus a bright line rule—is a very common type of policy argument for many tort rules.

Notes for Policy Answer

Arguments for bright line approach (minority rule)—

Arguments based on consequences/utilitarian:

Difficulty of proof
limited language facility of children
possible intimidation/fear in courtroom setting when called as witness

Institutional consideration
bright line rules easy; cut down on litigation

Arguments for case by case determination (majority rule)—

Argument based on fairness/deontological/rights analysis:
Persons ought to pay for damage they have caused
one purpose of tort law is to give compensation to those injured; here the plaintiff is clearly innocent, while the child may or may not be.

Argument based on consequences:
Deterrence
possible liability might make parents more watchful

Sample Question

Question

John, the personnel manager, and Jim, a job candidate, walked onto the elevator at Widget Company at 9:00 a.m. Standing in the corner of the elevator away from everyone else was Robert, who, as all employees of the company knew, had an abnormal fear of germs and never shook hands with anyone. John was in a playful mood and reached out to shake Robert's hand. Although Robert recoiled in horror, John grabbed his hand and greeted him heartily. Jim was not paying much attention to John's seemingly harmless behavior and did not see Robert lash out at John with his umbrella. John ducked and Robert hit the unsuspecting Jim on the head. Jim was knocked unconscious and fell to the floor of the elevator. Another person on the elevator—Bill—grabbed Robert's umbrella to prevent him from now attacking John. Most of the other people on the elevator worked on the 5th floor, so when the elevator stopped there, everyone pushed to get out. Sheila stepped on the unconscious Jim with her left foot as she attempted to leave the elevator. Discuss and analyze the potential tort liability of all parties.

Score Sheet

Legal theory:	
Battery as an issue	1
Robert v. John	
Elements of battery	
Intent	1
Contact	1
Harmful or offensive	1
Apply each:	
Volition	2
Intent to make contact	2
Discuss lack of purpose to harm or offend	3
Negate contact	1
Negate harmful or offensive	1
No defense	1
Jim v. Robert	
Identify possible battery between these parties	1
Elements of battery (no additional points for reciting elements again)	
Apply transferred intent	3
Apply contact	1
Apply harmful	1
Discuss whether offensive	2
No defense	1
Robert v. Bill	
Identify possible battery between these parties	1
Elements of battery (no additional points for reciting elements again)	
Apply volition	2
Apply intent to make contact	2
Discuss purpose to harm or offend	3
Defense of others—identify possible issue	1
Reasonable belief of need to defend	1
Apply	2
Minority rule—absolute vs. reasonable test	1
Apply	2
Proportional force	1
Apply	2

Jim v. Sheila

Identify possible battery between these parties	1
Elements of battery (no additional points for reciting elements again)	
Apply volition	2
Apply intent to make contact	2
Apply purpose to harm or offend	3
Defense (negate implied consent)	2
Total possible:	51

One important thing to note about this score sheet is that you must talk about all four party combinations. The points represent the maximum you could receive. No matter how wonderful your analysis of Robert v. John and Robert v. Bill, you can get at most 28 points if that's all you do. You need to be thorough but you also have to be efficient—speed in analysis and writing seems more important in torts exams than in any others.

It would be impossible to write a complete, in-depth answer to this question given the tight time constraints of law school exams. Below is an example of the kind of shortcut writing you may find necessary. Some professors will tell you not to discuss the elements not at issue. Although this sounds like an attractive suggestion, you will get no points if you have guessed wrong about the element at issue. You are probably safer having devoted at least one sentence to each of the elements even if you do not think they are at issue.

Answer

Battery requires that plaintiff demonstrate:
1. intent
2. contact
3. harmful or offensive

Robert v. John

(1) John may have had the requisite intent. He volitionally shook hands with Robert and meant to make contact. Normally shaking hands with a person would not demonstrate a purpose to harm or offend. But since the plaintiff's unusual sensitivity is known to defendant, we might infer the action was intended to offend.

(2) There was a contact ("grabbed Robert's hand").

(3)There is no evidence it was harmful according to an external standard, but it was arguably offensive ("Robert recoiled"). The usual test of offensiveness is an objective standard—what a reasonable person in the circumstances would find offensive. But in situations where the plaintiff's unusual sensitivity is known to the defendant, courts have found the action offensive.

Since John knew about Robert's fear (and there seems to be no defense), he would probably be liable for battery.

Jim v. Robert

(1) Robert seems to have the requisite intent. He volitionally "lashed out with an umbrella." That almost certainly means he had as his purpose to make contact. It may be harder to prove he had as his purpose to harm or offend, though "lashing out" raises the possibility that it was substantially certain that he would cause injury.

(2) There was contact ("Robert hit the unsuspecting Jim on the head").

(3) Even if not harmful (we don't know if there was enough pain or physical damage to count) it almost certainly would be considered offensive to a reasonable person. Although Robert intended to hit John, the doctrine of transferred intent applies. Robert might try to argue that this act was performed in self defense (since Jim had attacked him), but it is unlikely that this defense would be available since his striking out was not with force proportional to the threat.

Robert is probably liable to Jim.

Robert vs. Bill

(1) Bill's actions may or may not satisfy the element of intent. He volitionally grabbed the umbrella, and pretty clearly intended to make contact with the umbrella, but it is unclear and unlikely that he had as his purpose to harm or offend.

(2) Bill did not make contact with Robert's person. But he did grab the umbrella. In order for the element of contact to be satisfied, it is not necessary that Bill touch Robert. It is enough that he touch something "closely associated" to Robert, in this case his umbrella. Although the facts here do not have the racial overtones of *Fisher v. Carrousel Motor Hotel, Inc.* 424 S.W. 2d 627 (Tex. 1967), an umbrella in the hands of the plaintiff almost certainly meets the "close association" rule.

(3) There is no known physical harm to Robert—we are not told that his shoulder was dislocated, for example—but because Bill grabbed an object closely associated with him, it could be strongly argued that this would be offensive to Robert under the objective standard . However, Bill may assert the defense of others defense ("to prevent him from now attacking John"). A reasonable person in Bill's position could believe Robert might attack others. Robert would argue he directed his attack at the original person who touched him, and that in context there is no evidence he would attack others. The force Bill used ("grabbed Robert's um-

brella") seems small, and therefore proportional to even the arguably remote threat that Robert might attack someone else. Given this relatively small use of force by Bill, one might also argue that the grabbing would not be viewed as offensive to the reasonable person.

Bill therefore has more than one argument to avoid liability to Robert.

Jim v. Sheila

(1) Sheila acted volitionally. She may or may not have intended to step exactly where she did—thus intent to make contact might be at issue. Although there is no evidence that Sheila had a conscious desire to step on Jim, the requisite intent might be found. Given the large number of people getting off at one floor and an unconscious man on the elevator floor, Sheila might have known with substantial certainty that she would step on Jim or someone else. While she probably did not have as her purpose to harm or offend, it could be argued that harm or offense was substantially certain.

(2) The contact is clear ("stepped on Jim with her left foot").

(3) We do not know if there was any physical harm (a bruise or pain, perhaps?). Offensiveness, judged by a reasonable person standard, is a pretty strong argument—getting stepped on by someone in an elevator is likely to meet this test.

(4) Sheila might argue that courts usually hold that persons on a crowded elevator have impliedly consented to being touched. However, the scope of the consent would be limited to the occasional shove because of a lurching car or to pushing to get from the back of the car to the front. Most people would not believe that they had consented to being stepped on, and it is therefore probably unreasonable for Sheila to believe that such consent has been given.

As a result, Sheila probably would be liable to Robert.

Note that the answers above contain phrases like, "although it could be argued," and "the better argument is." These are useful fall-back exam phrases when you are arguing two sides of an issue. These formulations allow you to first set out a possible argument that you know is weak, and then allow you to counter it with an argument that you feel is stronger. Particularly if your professor wants you to present a conclusion, this allows a good transition to your conclusion.

Notice also that one fact—the grabbing of the umbrella—is relevant in at least two places in your answer. First, it goes to the issue of the "contact" (an object closely associated with Bill). Second, it goes to the proportionality of the force used in defense of others. This is a reminder that one fact can be used in more than one place, and also a reminder why it is advisable to organize your answer in a step-by-step manner, from the top down, rather than by merely seeing facts and trying to label their significance.

And finally, notice the use of the *Fisher v. Carrousel Motor Hotel, Inc.* case to argue by analogy—taking the facts of a decided case and arguing that the facts in front of us now make a stronger or weaker argument for finding the element.

Assault

Analysis Hints

Reading and practicing many questions will develop your ability to recognize key words in fact patterns that tell you an element of a tort is satisfied without saying so directly. For a defendant to be liable for assault, one of the elements that must be met is that the plaintiff must have had apprehension that an imminent battery-like contact might occur. Remember what we said earlier—the elements tell you what questions to ask of the fact pattern. So what should you be looking for to signal that apprehension? One common device is a word such as "ducked" or "flinched." If someone ducks or flinches, he must have seen something to be avoided—an imminent battery-like contact. This opens the door to a possible assault. You also need to show that the apprehension is reasonable, as well as the other elements of assault. But if you don't pay attention to the word "ducked" in two questions in this section, you will miss the tort of assault altogether.

Also, in the suggested draft outline, we are going to give you a couple of examples of what we mean when we say that your outline should capture everything you have learned. Just because we haven't put every such point in every sample outline doesn't mean *your* outline shouldn't be trying to capture these sub-elements, grey areas, and common arguments.

Draft Outline

Rule: Liability for assault requires the plaintiff show that defendant has:

1. **Intent**

   Subjective purpose to cause apprehension (or to commit a battery, using the Restatement's "interchangeable intent" idea)[4]

---

4. But remember, the subjective purpose test for assault can be demonstrated directly or by substantial certainty. And we can also use the intent to commit a battery (the interchangeable intent idea from the Restatement) or use transferred intent from the other trespassory torts.

2. An **Act**

   The traditional rule is that "mere words are not enough."[5]

3. That causes **Apprehension**

   Judged subjectively (was this plaintiff apprehensive?)

   Judged objectively (would a reasonable person have apprehension of a battery-like contact in such a situation?)[6]

4. Of an **Imminent**

5. **Battery-like contact** (some professors and hornbooks will just say "battery")

6. (Then, after analyzing each and every element of the prima facie case, discuss any) **Defenses.**

   The most likely would be self-defense or defense of others.

This first sample question is pretty straightforward. Since all elements are clearly satisfied, your task is to write a short summary paragraph.

---

5. This is an example of a gloss or definition that adds to what you know beyond merely stating the requirement of an act. If it was discussed in your class, it should be in your outline. Notice that it is not an element or even a sub-element. Rather, it addresses a common interpretation or grey area that arises around the "act" element. Most courts in most situations will require SOME physical act in addition to threatening words (for example, the raising of an arm, the pointing of a gun, etc.). We won't include a full discussion of this in the problems below, but always keep in mind these additional grey areas or common arguments related to a given element as you make your outline.

6. Your professor or reading may emphasize one aspect or another of this test, or both. This is a classic example of a sub-element or gloss or grey area. It goes beyond merely reciting the element—"apprehension." The subjective and objective tests tell us something else the legal system looks for in determining whether an assault occurred. If your professor mentions both tests, these become two separate steps in analysis. And therefore this *should be in your outline*. Remember, a key to having a good outline is to capture everything you know about the legal theory—in this case, the "apprehension" element of assault. In the sample questions below, for the sake of simplicity, we will only apply the subjective test (was this plaintiff in fact apprehensive?).

Sample Question

Question

John, Jim and Bill were playing with water pistols. Jim's aim was poor and Bill had been teasing him about it all afternoon. Finally Jim had had enough. He went up to Bill, waved his pistol in his face and aimed. Bill ducked. What torts?

Notes for Answer

Intent—"Bill had been teasing him ... finally Jim had had enough. He went up to Bill, waved his pistol in his face, and aimed"—we can infer his subjective intent or use substantial certainty.

Act—"waved his pistol in his face and aimed"

Caused Apprehension—"Bill ducked." Subjectively, Bill had apprehension. No reason to believe that Jim would **not** squirt the pistol at Bill, therefore a person in this situation would reasonably believe (objective test) that Jim would squirt him.

Imminent—water pistol is right in Bill's face; no threat of delayed retaliation such as "I'll deal with you later."

Battery-like Contact—being hit by water would be offensive, even if not harmful. Possible rebuttal? Since they were all playing earlier, in context it might not be offensive.

Possible Defense—in light of playing together earlier, maybe consent

Answer

Liability for assault requires that the defendant:

1. has intent (to cause apprehension)
2. commits an act
3. that causes apprehension by the plaintiff
4. of an imminent
5. battery-like contact
6. and there is no applicable defense

(1) Here, even if Jim would not admit it, we can infer he intended to cause apprehension. It might even be substantially certain—if a person points a water pistol at someone else in this manner it, is substantially certain that the other person will have apprehension.

(2) The pointing of the water pistol is the act.

(3) We know Bill was apprehensive—he saw something coming—because he ducked. And objectively, a person in this situation would be apprehensive.

(4) There clearly was the ability to squirt Bill immediately, and his ducking indicates he believed the battery-like contact would be imminent.

(5) Being squirted by water would certainly count as a battery-like contact (it is an extension of the defendant or something put in motion by the defendant). Unless John can get a jury to believe that he did not intend to cause apprehension on the part of Bill, he is likely to be liable.

(6) The fact that Jim was teased by Bill may have been the reason that Jim did what he did, but being provoked by teasing does not constitute a defense.

Up until now we have numbered each step of our analysis when we set down the elements and when we presented a sample answer. We won't do that throughout the book, but keep in mind why we have shown you this—to remind you that every question needs to be approached with a step-by-step method.

Practice Questions

The next question is a variation of the previous one. There are arguments on both sides about whether the element of "imminent" is satisfied. Cross out or underline the words we have used in the Notes for Answer as you go through the Question Copy, and then add any other analysis you have derived from your reading and class discussion to complete the answer we have started.

Question

John, Jim and Bill were playing with water pistols. Jim's aim was poor, and Bill had been teasing him about it all afternoon. Finally Jim had had enough. He went up to Bill, waved his pistol in his face and yelled, "If you don't stop teasing me I'll hit you with this." Bill immediately backed away. What torts?

Notes for Answer

Possible assault

1. **Intent**—"waved his pistol ... if you don't stop teasing me I'll hit you;" we can infer intent or find it with substantial certainty
2. **Act**—"went up to Bill", "waved his pistol in his face"
3. Caused **Apprehension**—"Bill immediately backed away"—subjective; in the situation a reasonable person would be apprehensive—objective
4. **Imminent**—this is the element most at issue

   argument for:

      proximity—went up to Bill and waved pistol in Bill's face, Bill backed away

   argument against:

      only if Bill didn't stop teasing him—conditional threat

The conditional threat *negates* the fact that he will be hit immediately

If imminence is found, the fact that the plaintiff could avoid the battery by stopping the teasing would not change the liability of Jim—the defendant can't force the plaintiff to stop lawful behavior (teasing) with threat of harm

5. **Battery-like Contact**—being hit would be harmful and offensive
6. with no valid **Defense**

Beginning of Answer

Liability for assault requires that the plaintiff demonstrate:

1. Intent
2. Act
3. Apprehension
4. Imminent
5. Battery-like Contact
6. with no Defense

Defendant Jim would be liable if he had the requisite intent for assault, and did some act that caused apprehension of an imminent battery-like contact. Here, it is fair to infer that Jim intended to cause apprehension (he "went up to" Bill in response to teasing). There is absolutely no evidence to the contrary (such as him claiming that he was just showing Bill his new water pistol), and we can also probably use substantial certainty (it is almost certain someone would be apprehensive in such a situation, therefore we can conclude that John intended that result). He committed an act ("went up to" him and "waved his pistol in his face") which caused apprehension ("Bill immediately backed away"). That apprehension would be reasonable under the circumstances—apparent retaliation for being teased, with no evidence that Jim was unwilling to hit Bill. If he hit Bill, that would obviously be a battery-like contact. The element most at issue is whether Jim threatened an imminent contact. Jim would argue that he made only a conditional threat, which negates the imminence element. Bill would argue in response ...

Question Copy

John, Jim and Bill were playing with water pistols. Jim's aim was poor, and Bill had been teasing him about it all afternoon. Finally Jim had had enough. He went up to Bill, waved his pistol in his face and yelled, "If you don't stop teasing me I'll hit you with this." Bill immediately backed away. What torts?

Once more we remind you that the same fact can help satisfy more than one element. That's one reason why you don't want to organize your answer around the facts. Rather, you want to organize your answer around the elements, fitting the facts of a new problem or exam question to the rules.

The following question appeared earlier in the Battery section. Here we have added the notes for the assault issues. Like many multi-tort, multi-party questions, this one does not tax your analytical abilities for most of the elements, just your ability to find all the assaults and write about them quickly. You can use the same format you used for your answers in the battery section.

Question

John, the personnel manager, and Jim, a job candidate, walked onto the elevator at Widget Company at 9:00 a.m. Standing in the corner of the elevator away from everyone else was Robert, who, as all employees of the company knew, had an abnormal fear of germs and never shook hands with anyone. John was in a playful mood and reached out to shake Robert's hand. Although Robert recoiled in horror, John grabbed his hand and greeted him heartily. Jim was not paying much attention to John's seemingly harmless behavior and did not see Robert lash out at John with his umbrella. John ducked and Robert hit the unsuspecting Jim on the head. Jim was knocked unconscious and fell to the floor of the elevator. Another person on the elevator — Bill—grabbed Robert's umbrella to prevent him from now attacking John. Most of the other people on the elevator worked on the 5th floor, so when the elevator stopped there, everyone pushed to get out. Sheila stepped on the unconscious Jim with her left foot as she attempted to leave the elevator. Analyze and discuss any possible claims for assault.*

Notes for Answer — Assault

Robert v. John

Possible assault

1. Intent

   Subjective purpose to cause apprehension — but remember this can be demonstrated directly, by substantial certainty, or using transferred intent.

   Here, "everyone knew" Robert didn't like shaking hands, so if John in fact knew, we can infer he intended to cause apprehension in Robert, and perhaps that it was substantially certain that he would. If he didn't know, hard to prove subjective intent.

2. Act

   Here, John reached out to shake hands.

---

* Of course there are also possible batteries—you may wish also to practice answering as if the call of the question were "discuss and analyze all torts."

3. Apprehension—judged subjectively (was this plaintiff apprehensive?)

   Here, Bill "recoiled in horror."

   Notice—the fact that a reasonable person might not find it offensive does NOT negate the fact that Bill subjectively had apprehension (if that is the only test).

   Instead, the fact that Bill is hypersensitive goes more to John's intent (did he have as his purpose to harm or offend?), and possibly to negating the conclusion that the contact would even be considered a battery-like contact. Each element has to be dealt with separately.

4. Imminent

   Here, John's hand is suddenly reaching out, and they are very close to each other

5. Battery-like Contact

   Here, the contact would be battery-like (while perhaps not harmful or offensive judged by reasonable person standard, since John knows Bill will find it offensive it counts as a battery). If John did not know of Bill's hypersensitivity, then the contact likely does not meet the objective standard of offensiveness, and cannot be considered harmful.

6. Defenses.

   The most likely would be self-defense or defense of others.

John v. Robert

Possible assault

1. Intent

   Subjective purpose to cause apprehension—hard to show even using inference or substantial certainty. But because there is intent to commit a battery, John can use transferred intent.

2. Act

   The lashing out

3. Apprehension

   John ducked

4. Imminent

   Yes, they were in close proximity

5. Battery-like Contact

   Being hit would be offensive and probably also harmful

6. Defenses

   The most likely would be self-defense or defense of others.

Jim v. Robert

Possible assault

Robert v. Bill

Possible battery

Possible assault

Jim v. Sheila

Possible battery

Possible assault

Question Copy

John, the personnel manager, and Jim, a job candidate, walked onto the elevator at Widget Company at 9:00 a.m. Standing in the corner of the elevator away from everyone else was Robert, who, as all employees of the company knew, had an abnormal fear of germs and never shook hands with anyone. John was in a playful mood and reached out to shake Robert's hand. Although Robert recoiled in horror, John grabbed his hand and greeted him heartily. Jim was not paying much attention to John's seemingly harmless behavior and did not see Robert lash out at John with his umbrella. John ducked and Robert hit the unsuspecting Jim on the head. Jim was knocked unconscious and fell to the floor of the elevator. Another person on the elevator—Bill—grabbed Robert's umbrella to prevent him from now attacking John. Most of the other people on the elevator worked on the 5th floor, so when the elevator stopped there, everyone pushed to get out. Sheila stepped on the unconscious Jim with her left foot as she attempted to leave the elevator. Analyze and discuss any possible claims for assault.[7]

7. Of course there are also possible batteries—you may also wish to practice answering as if the call of the question were "discuss and analyze all torts."

False Imprisonment

Draft Outline

Rule: Liability for false imprisonment requires that the plaintiff demonstrate on the part of the defendant:

1. **Intent**

   Subjective test—to confine

2. Act of **Confinement**

   Act by defendant—physical confinement

   Or possibly coercive situation—exercise of authority (for example, being ordered to "stay here" by a security guard, teacher, etc.)

   The confinement is negated if plaintiff could, without harm, escape

3. For some minimal period of **Time**
4. **Space**

   In a bounded or specific area or

5. With the plaintiff **Aware** of the confinement (*or* suffering actual physical harm if not aware)
6. Without privilege or consent

   Some courts list this as an element, but consent is technically a **Defense**, not an element of the prima facie case.

Sample Question

Question

John, the personnel manager of Widget Company, walked onto the company elevator at 9:00 a.m. Standing in the corner, away from everyone else, was Robert. Almost everyone knew that Robert had an abnormal fear of germs. He never shook hands with anyone. John had just learned that Robert had filed a complaint about him with the company president, and he decided to make things miserable for Robert. He suddenly reached out to shake Robert's hand. Although Robert recoiled in horror, John grabbed his hand and greeted him heartily. Robert lashed out at John and hit him with his umbrella. John was stunned but not hurt. Bill, a new Widget Company security guard who was also on the elevator, refused to let Robert get off the elevator when it got to Robert's floor. They rode up two more floors, and the guard told Robert to follow him to the security office. Once there, the security supervisor told Bill about Robert's phobia, apologized, and told Robert that he was free to go. Robert sued the security guard for false imprisonment. What result?

Notes for Answer

1. **Intent**

   Here, the guard acted in a way that has no explanation other than that he had as his purpose to keep Robert on the elevator and then intended to lead him to the security office.

2. **Confinement**

   Here, TWO separate acts of confinement

   The first—"refused to let Robert get off the elevator"

   The second—leading Robert to the security office

   Notice—we are not told security guard ever touched Robert

   But assertion of authority, and possibility of punishment for failing to comply, can count as confinement, if a reasonable person would feel obligated to stay

   Actual use of force or threat of force not necessary

3. **Time**

   Small amount of time, especially on the elevator, but enough to satisfy the element

4. Bounded **Space** or specific area

   Here, the elevator

   Robert is also forced by the guard to accompany him to the security office

5. **Awareness** by plaintiff (or actual harm if not aware)

   Clearly met here

6. After discussing each element of the prima facie case, you would then discuss any possible **Defenses**

   Defense of others (possibly)

   We need to know whether Robert was still attacking John

   And even if he had stopped, did security guard have reasonable belief that Robert might attack someone else?

   Discipline

   Normally applies to school teacher situation

   If a court is willing to apply it to employment situation, it might work here

Answer

Liability for false imprisonment requires that the defendant intends to confine, and commits an act that confines the plaintiff for at least some small amount of time in a specific or bounded area. There is no question that Bill caused Robert to be confined in a bounded area intentionally. He "refused to let Robert get off the elevator."

However, he has a defense, the defense of others. Bill saw Robert hit John for no apparent reason. As a security guard he is charged with the safety of Widget employees. Therefore, he would be obligated to detain someone who did attack one employee and might attack others. Bill would not be liable to Robert for false imprisonment.

Underline or cross out the words used in the Notes for Answer in the copy of the question below. Expand the notes from your class and case notes and then write your own answer to the question.

Question Copy

John, the personnel manager of Widget Company, walked onto the company elevator at 9:00 a.m. Standing in the corner, away from everyone else, was Robert. Almost everyone knew that Robert had an abnormal fear of germs. He never shook hands with anyone. John had just learned that Robert had filed a complaint about him with the company president, and he decided to make things miserable for Robert. He suddenly reached out to shake Robert's hand. Although Robert recoiled in horror, John grabbed his hand and greeted him heartily. Robert lashed out at John and hit him with his umbrella. John was stunned but not hurt. Bill, a new Widget Company security guard who was also on the elevator, refused to let Robert get off the elevator when it got to Robert's floor. They rode up two more floors, and the guard told Robert to follow him to the security office. Once there, the security supervisor told Bill about Robert's phobia, apologized, and told Robert that he was free to go. Robert sued the security guard for false imprisonment. What result?

Intentional Infliction of Severe Emotional Distress

Draft Outline

Liability for intentional infliction of severe emotional distress requires that the defendant:

1. Have **Intent** to cause severe emotional distress—subjective test

   But more modern view (Restatement Third) allows intent to be met by "reckless" behavior by defendant, which is easier to prove than subjective intent

   Transferred intent from other intentional torts *cannot* be used

2. Commit an **Extreme and Outrageous Act**
3. That causes **Severe Emotional Distress**

Notice that, for several of the intentional torts, causation is not listed as a separate element, because it is usually inherent in the fact pattern. For example, if someone punches someone else in the nose (a battery) it's pretty obvious that the punch caused the injury. But with emotional harm, the link between defendant's action and the plaintiff's claimed distress is not so clear, and needs to be proven (and is therefore treated as a separate, explicit element). For example, a bill collector might arguably have acted in an outrageous manner, and caused severe emotional distress. But if the plaintiff was already upset about losing her job, it may be the layoff and not the bill collector that is the cause of her distress.

Two sub-elements to keep in mind:

a. most courts don't require expert witnesses or medical evidence; the jury is allowed to draw its own conclusions in most cases based on their common sense

b. the more outrageous the conduct, the more likely the jury is to believe that it was the defendant that caused the emotional harm.

This raises another point about emotional harm claims. As with all torts, each element must be separately analyzed, and each one must be demonstrated to make out the prima facie case. But for this tort the elements are much more *inter-related.* The more outrageous the conduct, the more likely we are to believe it caused the harm AND the more likely we are to believe that the defendant intended to inflict that harm. And it goes the other way as well—the more severe the resulting emotional harm, the more likely we are to characterize the conduct as outrageous.

After you do your step-by-step analysis of each element, it is always useful to step back and consider any other factors that might push the court in one direction or the other. But for this tort, it is also useful to show that you understand that the elements are interrelated.

Sample Question

Question

John, the personnel manager of Widget Company, walked onto the company elevator at 9:00 a.m. Standing in the corner, away from everyone else, was Robert. Almost everyone knew that Robert had an abnormal fear of germs. He never shook hands with anyone. John had just learned that Robert had filed a complaint about him with the company president, and he decided to make things miserable for Robert. He suddenly reached out to shake Robert's hand. Although Robert recoiled in horror, John grabbed his hand and greeted him heartily. Robert was so upset that he suffered a migraine headache which kept him out of work for two days. Robert sued John for intentional infliction of severe emotional distress. What result?

Notes for Answer

1. Intent to cause

   Subjective test of defendant's purpose

   Also includes reckless behavior under Restatement Third

   Argument for:

   Intended Robert to be upset—"decided to make things miserable for Robert"

2. Extreme and outrageous conduct ("conduct that transcends all bounds of decency")

   Arguments for:

   Knew of Robert's sensitivity

   Grabbed his hand in front of many people in the elevator

   Argument against:

   Although perhaps immature and ill-mannered, not outrageous

3. Caused severe emotional distress

   Arguments for:

   "So upset"

   Migraine headache

   Lashed out at John

Answer

Liability for intentional infliction of severe emotional distress requires that the defendant:

1. intended to cause severe emotional distress
2. did something extreme and outrageous
3. that caused severe emotional distress

Intent—Here, John intended "to make things miserable for Robert." Knowing of Robert's sensitivity, John at least behaved recklessly (which satisfies the Restatement Third test). It can be strongly argued that John subjectively had as his purpose to cause severe emotional distress.

Outrageous conduct—Here, the issue of outrageous conduct is in dispute. John's behavior was certainly ill-mannered or even immature, but shaking someone's hand does not seem to rise to the level of extreme and outrageous conduct. However, courts have held that, when a party knows of another's sensitivity, conduct intended to upset can be considered outrageous.

Caused severe emotional distress—He "upset" Robert, causing a migraine headache and a violent reaction. There is no evidence that other things happened to cause the distress, so it is at least possible if not likely for a jury to conclude that this incident caused the distress. The migraine headache may or may not rise to the level of severe, depending how the court interprets that requirement. If a jury believes John intended to upset Robert, they may take the more expansive view of severe and find the element met. So it is possible that John would be liable for the intentional infliction of severe emotional distress.

Underline or cross out the words used in the Notes for Answer in the Question Copy below. Expand them from your class and case notes, and then write your own answer to the question. Notice that the same fact—John's knowledge of Robert's sensitivity—is relevant to two different elements—the outrageousness of the conduct *and* John's intent (purpose). Again this reminds us to *first* do a step-by-step, top-down analysis, and *then* do a bottom-up analysis, double-checking to see if any fact suggests something we haven't already addressed.

Question Copy

John, the personnel manager of Widget Company, walked onto the company elevator at 9:00 a.m. Standing in the corner, away from everyone else, was Robert. Almost everyone knew that Robert had an abnormal fear of germs. He never shook hands with anyone. John had just learned that Robert had filed a complaint about him with the company president, and he decided to make things miserable for Robert. He suddenly reached out to shake Robert's hand. Although Robert recoiled in horror, John grabbed his hand and greeted him heartily. Robert was so upset that he suffered a migraine headache which kept him out of work for two days. Robert sued John for intentional infliction of severe emotional distress. What result?

Chapter 3

Negligence

Analysis Hints

The Two Meanings of "Negligence"

It can be confusing when someone uses the word "negligence" since it can have two meanings. The first meaning labels a cause of action or theory of recovery in tort—negligence as distinguished from an intentional tort or recovery based on strict liability. The second meaning applies to one element of the cause of action for negligence—negligence as a conclusion that the element of breach is met because the defendant failed to exercise the amount of care that was required in the situation. This failure to exercise due care leads to a successful cause of action for negligence if the other elements are also met. The rule for the tort of negligence then can be phrased as:

Rule: Liability for negligence requires that the defendant had a duty to the plaintiff to exercise a certain standard of care, breached that standard of care, and that the breach was the cause in fact and the legal cause of actual harm to the plaintiff.

The law considers our general duty to others is to not act in a way that will subject others to unreasonable harm. If we act negligently and someone is harmed, we may be liable for our conduct, unless we have some valid defense. Although any or all of the elements can be in play, the standard of care, the breach of that standard, and whether that breach was the legal cause of harm are probably at the heart of most negligence fact patterns.

Here is another way to think of the requirements for the tort of negligence:

Rule: the plaintiff must demonstrate that:

1. the defendant owed a **Duty** to the plaintiff;
2. there was a certain **Standard of Care** owed;
3. the defendant **Breached** (failed to meet) the standard of care;
4. the breach was the **Cause in Fact** (factual cause) of plaintiff's harm;
5. the breach was the **Legal** (proximate) cause of plaintiff's harm; and
6. the plaintiff suffered **Harm**

7. with no applicable **Defenses** (after discussing the prima facie case).

This step-by-step method emphasizes the point that issues of duty, standard of care, breach, and factual and legal causation are separate (even if, as we will discuss shortly, some courts treat duty issues as causation issues or vice versa).

The answers in the Sample Questions section show how this approach makes the task of writing your answer simpler.

In many common situations, the issue of whether the plaintiff was owed a duty is simple. If the defendant was driving down the street and swerving onto the sidewalk, and injured someone walking by, it would be clear that the defendant had a duty to the plaintiff (that was almost certainly breached). If the defendant was chopping down a tree near the edge of his property, and failed to warn a passerby who was hit on the head by the falling tree, it would be clear that the defendant had a duty to the plaintiff (that may or may not have been breached, depending on how careful the person chopping down the tree had been). In both cases, the defendant acted in a way that endangered some other person or persons. The duty to the plaintiff was owed by virtue of the fact that both the plaintiff and defendant are members of society and that the actions of the defendant endangered the plaintiff. This is in contrast to what you study in your contracts class, where parties owe each other duties because they have voluntarily taken on some duty to another person (to fulfill whatever the promise is).

Note: Proximate Cause vs. Legal Cause

The majority of cases in your casebook may refer to element 5 in the list above as "proximate cause." The Restatement Section 431 uses the term "legal cause." While either term is correct (unless your professor says otherwise), we prefer to use the term "legal cause" for two reasons. First, it makes clear that these judgments are not empirical judgments but reflections of various rules and policies. Second, the term "proximate" can lead you to think that the most important distinction the courts draw is between injuries that are close in space and time to the act of breach and those that are not. While these factors can be taken into account in deciding cases, there are all sorts of other rules and factors used by courts that have nothing to do with whether the ultimate injury is "proximate" in space and time.

Also, you should be aware that some hornbooks, commercial outlines, and court opinions compress legal and factual cause into one element. Keep in mind that there are different tests and arguments for each of these. Whether you treat them in your outline as two sub-elements under the heading "cause" or as two separate elements is not as important as making sure you address each of them in your step-by-step analysis.

Remember we said earlier that different casebooks and readings list elements differently. Here's one more example. Many sources will not list the "standard of care" as a separate element. Some will lump it in with "duty" (for example, "defendant owed the plaintiff a duty of reasonable care"); others with "breach." Again, there is no right or wrong way to list elements. But note that the analysis of whether there is a duty owed is different from what the standard of care is for a particular type of defendant, which is different from how courts decide whether there is a breach. If there is a step in a legal analysis that is distinct from another step and involves different rules or factors, make sure you capture that in your outline—either by listing it as a separate element or by listing it as a sub-element. The key is to make sure you go through each separate step in your analysis.

Looking back at the two statements of the rule, can you see why, for most students, the second formulation is more useful? It is more useful because it spells out the precise steps in analysis that you must take, the precise elements that must be met. The first formulation, though correct and complete, blurs together steps that you will want to take to make certain you have addressed all possible issues in a potential negligence case (except for Defenses, which you would discuss after setting out all relevant elements of the prima facie case).

No Duty to Act

In most casebooks and commercial outlines there will be a subsection under the heading "Duty" with a statement such as, "The law imposes no affirmative duty to act." In some casebooks this topic won't come up until well after you have gone through all of the basic elements of negligence (including duty). This language is shorthand for a basic distinction within the category of duty. As mentioned above, by virtue of being members of society we have a duty to not create or cause danger to others by our careless actions. But in general we have no duty to come to the aid of others, or to act to protect others, when the underlying danger is coming from someone or something else. The classic example used in some discussions of this is the hypothetical person standing on a pier who sees someone drowning and could, with minimal effort and no danger to him or herself, throw a life preserver to the drowning person. While we may have a moral duty, conventional tort law says we have no legal duty. Even medical professionals have no duty to give aid. To encourage medical professionals and others to help the injured, many states have enacted "Good Samaritan" statutes to protect them from liability for anything but gross negligence.

There are, however, some instances in which a person does have a duty to act:

1. A person who helped cause a situation resulting in peril or harm to another person (even if it was a non-negligent act) has a duty to give aid to the person who is in danger or who has been injured.
2. A legislature can create a statutory duty to act that did not exist at common law and give the victim a specific right to recover.[1]
3. If a defendant undertakes to give aid to someone who has been harmed (even though there was no duty to do so), and in some way the person is worse off as a result of the defendant beginning to give aid, the defendant has a duty to continue to give aid. The most common instances of this would be:
    - if the victim relies on the fact that the defendant will continue giving aid;
    - if the victim is worse off because other potential rescuers are given an indication that they do not need to come to the victim's aid;
    - if the defendant does the rescue itself in a way that further injures or endangers the victim.
4. People with certain prior relationships to the victim may have a duty to give them aid or to protect them. Parents must aid their children; employers must aid their employees; employees of common carriers must aid their passengers. In some situations—a store owner protecting customers from a criminal or a landlord protecting tenants from a criminal—these are highly contested issues involving policy judgments.
5. People with a prior relationship to a bad person who injures the victim may have a duty to protect that victim. The classic case is that of a psychiatrist who knew of a specific threat to a specific victim and failed to take even minimal steps (such as warning the victim or the police). These situations depend on the knowledge of the defendant, their real or potential ability to control the bad person, as well as policy considerations.

---

1. If there is a statute that specifically creates a duty to act and gives the victim a right to recover, the person who failed to act may be liable. For example, many states have laws that require schoolteachers to report suspected incidents of child abuse. In most instances such a statute only provides some penalty for the teacher who fails to report (if the child continues to be abused). But the legislature *may* write the law in such a way that the victim (the abused child) can actually sue the teacher. In other words, the statute can create a duty that did not exist at common law, but most courts require fairly clear evidence that this is what the legislature intended.

The following fact pattern raises several examples where the potential defendant may or may not have had a duty to act.

Question

Janet and Bill were just married. They decided to go on their honeymoon to Snow Woods, one of the best ski resorts in the country. Janet was an expert skier, but Bill had only started skiing when he met Janet two years before. When they bought their lift tickets, the ticket seller said, "Be glad you weren't here yesterday. Man, was it crowded. We had our busiest day this season." Janet agreed to ski with Bill on the intermediate level trails in the morning and then leave him to go to the advanced level trails in the afternoon. Although there hadn't been much snow, they knew Snow Woods had great snowmaking equipment. The first run went well, so they decided to try the next most difficult intermediate trail, the very popular Owl View Trail.

As they approached the middle of the run, Bill suddenly was hit from behind by a novice skier for whom this trail was obviously beyond his capabilities. The skier continued on his way. Bill went sprawling. He screamed in pain as he tried to get up. Janet had been skiing behind Bill to help him improve his form. She immediately started towards Bill.

She saw someone they had met the night before at dinner skiing toward them. He was a physician with whom they had spent the evening discussing health care reform. She felt relief, but only momentarily. The physician looked right at Bill and then skied away. Janet arrived at Bill's side when two teenage boys stopped, took off their parkas and made a sling to carry Bill down the mountain. They didn't do a good job of it, and he slipped out of the sling, further damaging his foot. Who is liable to Bill?

In this fact pattern the physician had no duty to come to Bill's aid. This is an example of the general rule that a person has "no affirmative duty to act." The skier who hit Bill had the duty to give aid because he was the cause of the harm, even if he acted innocently. The teenagers had no duty to come to Bill's aid, but once they did, they had the duty to act reasonably. Arguments could be made on both sides as to whether they acted reasonably. You might say that they acted reasonably given their age and level of experience. However, teenagers might be expected to realize that getting a member of the rescue patrol or someone more skilled would have been the better approach.

The people who had a duty to come to Bill's aid would be liable for negligence if they didn't come to his aid, and all who did would be liable for negligence if they gave that aid in a negligent fashion. Notice that all of these potential defendants are characters in the fact pattern. Because they don't have names, it might be easy to overlook one or more of them (especially the skier who caused the initial accident, since you might have focused on the duty to aid after the injury). Notice something else—there may be another potential defendant that you could entirely overlook: the owner of the Snow Woods ski resort. Always be on the lookout for a "phantom" party—one that isn't even mentioned. While it is unlikely that the phantom defendant is the most important one your professor wants to discuss, spotting the phantom may also earn you points. In this case, Snow Woods might have a duty to provide sufficient ski patrols, or perhaps even to take steps to insure that novices don't go on the more difficult trails. We don't have enough facts to decide the resort's liability, but we do have enough facts to raise the possibility.

Special Policy Considerations

It can often be difficult to understand why a particular court has decided a case based on the element at issue being "duty" (did this defendant owe a duty to this foreseeable plaintiff?) and not based on "legal" or "proximate cause" (was this a foreseeable consequence of the defendant's breach?). It is comforting to note that the famous judges in Palsgraf disagreed on this very point. In that case, a railroad employee's negligent behavior caused a passenger to drop a package which happened to contain fireworks. When they exploded, weighing scales fell on Mrs. Palsgraf, who was thirty feet from the explosion. Cardozo, writing for the court, characterized the case as a duty case (Mrs. Palsgraf a foreseeable plaintiff). Andrews, in dissent, characterized the case as a proximate cause case (Mrs. Palsgraf's injury a foreseeable consequence).

If you read a case in your casebook in the legal or proximate cause section and you think it should be in the duty section, remember that Cardozo, one of the greatest common law judges ever, might have placed it in a different section. If Cardozo and Andrews couldn't agree on an analysis, what can be expected from a lesser judge or from ourselves? Your professor might give you some indication as to which is the preferred method of analysis. If not (and perhaps even if she does) you should try to show on an exam that you understand both ways of conceptualizing the case.

The importance of the concepts of duty and legal cause is that they provide limits to the scope of a defendant's liability. Even if the defendant has acted carelessly (breached), we might not want to hold him or her responsible to every conceivable person for every conceivable injury. The cases in your casebook may reflect strong policy considerations underlying the courts' decisions as to where to draw the line. Sometimes the policy is explicitly revealed by the court. But other times the opinion is written as if the decision had been based on a very objective analysis. The highly debatable nature of where to draw the line, and the intersection of law and policy, make duty and legal or proximate cause fact patterns common, especially if your professor has presented a particular approach to such issues.

Draft Outline for Negligence

1. **Duty**
   a. General duty to not endanger others by one's actions
   b. No duty to act to protect or aid others
      Unless one of the exceptions is met:
      1. Helped cause
      2. Statute
      3. Undertaking to rescue or assist and making the victim worse off
      4. Certain prior relationships between plaintiff and defendant—especially but not limited to recognized special relationships
      5. Certain prior relationships between the defendant and the "bad actor" (the person who caused the injury to the plaintiff)
2. **Standard of Care**
   a. To exercise the degree of care that the reasonable person would exercise in the circumstances (objective standard)
      1. Circumstances can include emergency
      2. Circumstances can include utilizing superior intelligence, knowledge, or experience (doesn't change the standard—reasonable person in the circumstances)
   b. Mental impairment (a less intelligent person, or even a mentally ill person)—objective standard (even though the person may not be able to meet it)
   c. Physical impairment—more subjective standard (a reasonable person with that impairment or limitation)
      Which might mean not engaging in the activity at all
   d. Professionals—held to a different standard than mere reasonableness
   e. Children—(more subjective standard)
      1. Judged by the degree of care that would be exercised by children of like age, intelligence, education and experience (partially subjective standard)
      2. Possible exception (some courts, some situations)—
         Children engaged in an activity normally engaged in by adults and that is dangerous
         If so, held to the same standard as an adult (objective)

f. Owners and Occupiers of Land[2]

Traditional rule—duty depends on classification of the plaintiff

1. Trespasser—limited or no duty
2. Invitee—some duty
3. Licensee—reasonable person standard

But special exceptions—known trespassers, children (attractive nuisance doctrine)

Modern trend—combine the three categories into two, or treat all cases as governed by "reasonable under the circumstances"

3. **Breach**—ways of discussing whether defendant breached the standard of care:
   a. General sense of the jury/"ad hoc" argument
   b. Violation of custom
      Can be some evidence of breach
      Compliance does not negate breach
      More significant if it is a safety custom
   c. Violation of the defendant's own standard (internal guidelines, manuals, etc)
      Can be some evidence of breach
      Compliance does not negate breach
      More significant if it is a safety standard
   d. Learned Hand test—comparing the burden (cost) to the defendant to avoid the harm (B) against the probability of harm (P) and the severity of the harm if something bad does occur (L)
      Is B>PL? If so, defendant is not negligent
   e. Negligence per se—establishes the standard of care (behavior specified by the statute) and the breach (violation of the statute)
      The court decides whether to apply a statute enacted for some other purpose to "borrow" for establishing tort liability
      The plaintiff must demonstrate—
      1. A statute—a state criminal statute is the clearest case (many courts will use negligence per se with a local ordinance or federal, state or local regulation)
         The statute must be one that provides a criminal penalty
      2. The statute must set a specific standard of behavior (not just duplicate a "reasonableness" standard)
      3. The violation must be unexcused
      4. The purpose of the statute is related to this situation and judged by two-pronged test:
         i. The type of harm intended to be sanctioned
         ii. The class of people intended to be protected

2. The treatment of duties owed by occupiers of land varies widely by jurisdiction and by professor. This is only a very basic outline.

(Many cases will raise the issue of how narrowly or broadly the court should interpret the purpose or purposes of the statute in deciding whether or not to apply it for tort liability)

Consequence if negligence per se applies:

Some courts—"automatic" finding of breach

Some courts—presumption of breach or some evidence of breach

f. Permissible inference without direct proof—res ipsa loquitur

4. **Cause in Fact/Factual Cause**
   a. "But-for"
   b. "Alternative Causes" which would otherwise be precluded by "but-for"
   c. "Substantial Factor" test
   d. "Loss of a chance"

5. **Legal (Proximate) Cause**

   Risk rule—Was this a foreseeable harm of the sort that made the defendant's action a breach?

   If there was no intervening cause:
   - a. Define the scope of the risk in narrow terms—what were the most foreseeable bad outcomes (arguing for the defendant)?
   - b. Define the scope of the risk in broad terms—what were plausibly foreseeable bad outcomes (arguing for the plaintiff)?

     (Reasonably foreseeable means using foresight, not merely "conceivable" in hindsight)

   Additional ways courts think about the risk rule:
   - a. Was this type/class of plaintiff foreseeable?

     This relates to the duty/legal cause debate discussed earlier between Cardozo and Andrews
   - b. Was the type of injury foreseeable?
   - c. Was the way the injury occurred foreseeable?

     Usually it doesn't matter how it occurred

   Intervening Causes

   Some other act that triggered or combined with the original act of negligence to cause the bad outcome

   If the intervening cause is foreseeable, the original defendant is still liable

   If the intervening act is not forseeable, the original defendant is not liable

   There may be joint and several liability with the intervening actor

   Negligent actions of an intervening actor are deemed to be foreseeable, including:

   Negligent medical care

   Negligent rescue

   Some acts are normally deemed to be unforeseeable, including:

   Criminal acts, intentional tortious acts, and reckless acts (but there are exceptions)

These acts are called "superseding" because they weren't foreseeable or because they were actions of an independent moral actor
Also considered unforeseeable—"Acts of God"/nature
Common counterargument for arguably superseding acts: exposing plaintiff to a criminal act or act of nature might in itself be negligent and therefore the criminal act or act of nature does not supersede

6. **Harm/Injury**
   Usually obvious in a fact pattern, but should not be overlooked
7. **Defenses**
   a. Contributorily negligent behavior by plaintiff
      Judged by the same tests used to judge a defendant
      Some jurisdictions don't hold certain plaintiffs (children, mentally incompetent) to the same objective standard used to judge a normal adult defendant

      Significance of contributorily negligent behavior:
      i. Traditional rule—complete bar to recovery
      ii. Modern approach (by court or statute)—comparative fault or comparative responsibility
          Plaintiff's recovery reduced by percentage of fault or responsibility
          "Pure" vs. "Modified"

   b. Assumption of risk
      Sometimes called "true" or "secondary" assumption of risk
      i. Knowledge/appreciation of risk (subjective test)
      ii. Voluntary confronting of the risk
      iii. Capacity

      Significance of assumption of risk:
      Traditional rule—complete bar to recovery
      Under comparative negligence express assumption of risk is a complete bar
      Implied assumption of risk treated the same as comparative negligence

Sample Questions

The questions in this section will concentrate on only one contested element of negligence at a time, with one exception. In those situations where there may be a special standard of care because of the category of duty owed (for example, occupiers of land), we have combined the traditional elements of "duty" and "standard of care" because some jurisdictions have moved away from many of the rules that called for different standards of care for different plaintiffs. This will allow you to practice discussing jurisdictional differences. Although you may find other elements of negligence suggested in any fact pattern, we will give analyses and answers for the only one element at issue. At the end of the chapter, you may want to go back and expand on your answers with analyses of other elements. Remember, almost any case or problem, even if it focuses on only one element, can be used as a review of the other elements. And in a complete answer on an exam, you should at least note each element and how it is satisfied, even if that element is not in dispute (unless your professor has indicated otherwise or the call of the question clearly asks for discussion of only one element). Finally, you should remember that although we are only addressing one element per question, many professors like to craft a question that has more than one debatable element.

This book gives you just a sampling of the kinds of analyses required in negligence cases. Most of the fact patterns in this chapter are based on a real case. We have presented the arguments from the case and written the sample answer so that the result matches the court's conclusion. However, your professor may have a different perspective than the court in question. After you have read our answer, review your notes from class and/or discuss the question with your study group before writing your answer. It goes without saying that you will have a better answer if you have taken into account the approach taken by your professor. After we present a fact pattern-based question, an outline of the answer, and a sample of an answer written out, we then give you the question again—the Question Copy—to allow you to practice your skills in relating the facts to the law. You may want to try setting out your own version of the answer in outline form, and writing your answer out, before looking at ours. But once you have looked at our sample outline and answer, we give you this second opportunity to use your notes based on your professor and class to write out your version of an answer.

Duty and Standard of Care

The general rule is that we owe a duty to not endanger others who could be foreseeably harmed by our negligent behavior. As discussed earlier, some courts and professors include the idea of "foreseeable plaintiffs" to whom duty is owed at this stage of analysis, while others deal with these issues under legal cause. Regardless of this duty vs. legal cause dispute, there are traditionally categories where the law imposes no duty (or only a limited duty) rather than the general duty judged by the reasonable person standard. The duty owed by possessors of land to those who come onto the property is the most common example. And there are other situations where the law imposes a special or higher duty. Common carriers are one example of this. In all cases, whether there is a duty is a matter of law to be decided by the judge.

Traditionally a landowner (or other possessor of land) owed no duty to a trespasser (or only owes a duty to avoid willful and wanton conduct). Under this rule, which some jurisdictions still follow, if a defendant can convince the judge that the plaintiff was a trespasser, it is irrelevant that the defendant failed to exercise the care that a reasonable person would have exercised. The defendant wins because of the category we place the plaintiff in, not because of any arguments about the behavior of the defendant.

Question

Mrs. Jones was moving, and her supply of packing boxes was completely depleted. She headed for her neighborhood supermarket where the store manager told her to go to the back room and take whatever boxes she needed. When she had picked up all she could carry, she noticed that there was a door open to the loading ramp in the back of the supermarket. Since her car was only a few feet away from this exit, she decided that it would be easier to go out that way than go all the way through the crowded store and then around to the back. However, as she went onto the loading dock she tripped on the poorly maintained ramp that the store manager had planned to repair. She broke her ankle. In a suit for negligence brought by Mrs. Jones against the store, what result?

Notes for Answer

Arguable negligence by the store owner

1. Duty
   Argument against:
   - Mrs. Jones a trespasser on the loading dock
   - Had permission to go into the back room, exceeded permission by going to the loading dock

   Argument for:
   - Mrs. Jones at least a licensee—on the premises with permission
   - Probably not a business invitee (at least if defined narrowly), since she is not there for the benefit of the store owner
   - Reasonable and foreseeable that she would exit from the loading dock
2. Standard of care
   If Mrs. Jones is a licensee, store must warn her of dangerous conditions known to them (the (poorly maintained ramp)
   If trespasser, no duty or only duty to avoid willful and wanton conduct
3. Breach
   Didn't warn

Answer

Liability for negligence requires that the plaintiff demonstrate:

Duty—owed to the plaintiff
Standard of care—normally reasonable person, but with many sub-rules
Breach
Cause in fact
Legal cause
Harm
With no applicable Defenses

Duty—If the jurisdiction uses the traditional categories, the duty owed will depend on which category the plaintiff fits into. In jurisdictions that do not use these categories, there is a general duty owed and the standard of care would be "reasonable under the circumstances".

Applying the traditional rules, the store will argue that Mrs. Jones was a trespasser on the loading dock. A trespasser is one who is on the land of another without permission. Although it is clear that she had the right to be in the back room, that right did not extend to the loading dock. When she went to the loading dock she exceeded her permission and her category changed from licensee to trespasser. If she is a trespasser, she is owed no duty (or perhaps the only duty she is owed is for the defendant to avoid willful and wanton behavior). Therefore, it would be irrelevant that there was a dangerous condition on the premises that they could have warned her about, and the store would have no liability for her injuries.

The court might apply the limited duty owed to a trespasser—a duty to avoid willful and wanton conduct. Here, the failure to warn her of a poorly maintained ramp is probably not willful or wanton, but it could be debated. We would need to know more to determine this—was the problem a slight irregularity in the surface of the ramp or some extremely dangerous condition, and did they have actual knowledge that she was about to confront the dangerous situation?

Even in a jurisdiction using the traditional categories, the plaintiff's attorney could argue that Mrs. Jones should be considered at least a licensee. A licensee is a person who has permission to enter the premises. In this case Mrs. Jones was told by the store manager to "go to the back room and take whatever boxes she needed." Therefore, she would be considered a licensee at least for the back room. In most jurisdictions the store has the duty to a licensee to make reasonable efforts to warn of a dangerous condition that the licensee is otherwise unlikely to discover. Since it would be foreseeable that someone in the back room would take the shortest route out of the store, it was foreseeable that Mrs. Jones would exit by way of the loading dock. Since the defendant knew that she would be laden down with boxes, this foreseeability is even higher. Therefore, the store manager had the duty to warn her of the problem with the loading dock. The store had a duty to Mrs. Jones as a licensee to warn her of known defects, and would be liable in negligence if the other elements are established and assuming the store manager knew of the danger.

In some jurisdictions the distinctions between classifications of people who enter the land have been abolished. There is then a general duty owed to all who come on the property, judged by the standard of a reasonable possessor of property. The plaintiff would argue that the conduct of the store manager was not reasonable.... The defendant would argue that his conduct was reasonable....

Question Copy

Mrs. Jones was moving, and her supply of packing boxes was completely depleted. She headed for her neighborhood supermarket where the store manager told her to go to the back room and take whatever boxes she needed. When she had picked up all she could carry, she noticed that there was a door open to the loading ramp in the back of the supermarket. Since her car was only a few feet away from this exit, she decided that it would be easier to go out that way than go all the way through the crowded store and then around to the back. However, as she went onto the loading dock she tripped on the poorly maintained ramp that the store manager had planned to repair. She broke her ankle. In a suit for negligence brought by Mrs. Jones against the store, what result?

Breach

You will probably be exposed to the Learned Hand formula (B<PL) in your discussions in class about what constitutes a breach of duty. This formula reflects the reality that deciding what a defendant should reasonably have done to prevent harm to someone like the plaintiff is usually a balancing of factors. It reflects the commonsense notion that if the possibility of a bad outcome is unlikely, or if the bad outcome would result in a relatively small amount of damage, we would not expect an actor in the defendant's position to expend as much time or effort in care. But the defendant WILL be considered to have breached if the burden (B) of preventing the harm was less than the probability of the harm (P) times the severity of the loss if something bad did happen (L). The formula is not intended to involve mathematical precision. Depending on the facts given, you may only be able to say that something was "very likely" or very unlikely." Or, in some situations, you may be able to be more precise—"the facts indicate that when left unattended, there was a one in four

chance that the car could roll down the hill." As mentioned in the sample outline earlier, there are several other ways courts analyze breach, and your readings or class discussions may suggest others. After answering the following question using the Learned Hand approach, you might want to practice applying other approaches.

Question

John, age 4, was playing in the playground of his nursery school with his older brother and his friends, who had no school on the day in question. Billie Brown has owned and operated the nursery school for many years. The older children decided to pretend to be knights in a dueling contest and went to the wooded area adjacent to the playground to get some sticks. It did not take long for the game to get out of hand, and John was hit in the eye by a stick thrown by one of the other boys. John's parents sued Billie Brown on behalf of John. What result?

Notes for Answer

Arguably negligence by the school owned by Billie Brown

1. **Duty**[3]

School has duty to protect students on its property while school is in session

2. **Breach**

Nature of the breach:

Nursery school owner knew wooded area had sticks that might be dangerous in the hands of children, therefore foreseeable

To remedy this dangerous condition, a reasonable nursery school operator should have provided supervision or fenced in the area to keep the playground free from sticks

Argument based on Learned Hand test:

Burden—
More supervision of playground (additional personnel at some cost) or fence (cost to install and maintain) to make sure kids have no sticks

---

3. For purposes of answering the question, you should assume that the nursery school has some duty to protect its students while they are on nursery school property and during school hours.

You might want to come back later and practice an answer to the question of whether there is any duty owed in this situation—here we are assuming there is, and we are assuming that the standard to be met is "reasonable under the circumstances."

Probability—
Foreseeable/some likelihood that kids will get hurt
Fairly small probability (debatable) even of the slight injuries
Very small probability of the more severe injuries

Severity of loss—
Most injuries from sticks will be slight
A few will be severe — injury to an eye, serious wound, etc.

3. **Cause in Fact**

4. **Legal Cause**

5. **Harm**

6. With no applicable **Defenses**

Answer

Liability for negligence requires that the plaintiff demonstrate:

1. A duty
2. The standard of care
3. A breach
4. Cause in fact
5. Legal cause
6. Harm
7. With no applicable Defenses

It is assumed for purposes of this question that a nursery school has a duty to protect its students from harm on school property during school hours. That duty is assumed to include acting reasonably under the circumstances. The issue here is whether Mr. Brown breached that duty in failing to keep sticks out of the playground.

The plaintiff would argue that Billie Brown could have protected the young persons in the playground from harm by fencing in the playground and/or by providing supervision so that sticks from the wooded area would not be used on the playground. However, Billie Brown is not required to prevent all harm. He must exercise the care that a reasonable person would have exercised to prevent foreseeable harm to someone like the plaintiff. Using the Learned Hand formula (breach if $B<PL$) to assess Mr. Brown's possible breach, it seems clear that the cost of providing a fence or providing greater supervision would both be significant expenditures. This cost of prevention — the burden part of the formula — must be less than the expected bad outcome—probability times the severity of harm—for us to consider the defendant's behavior to be a breach.

The mere cost of the fence may understate the true cost of prevention, since a normal fence is unlikely to keep the kids out. In addition, the children might use pencils or other objects at the school to fight with each other, so the fence may not be a viable option. The cost of the other most obvious method of preventing such injuries—more supervision—is likely to be great, as it would require enough teachers to keep a constant watch and to break up any dangerous play before someone is injured. Although there is a bad outcome here, and although it could be argued that kids playing with sticks may sometimes foreseeably injure each other, the likelihood of a serious injury is fairly low (kids play like this all the time and seldom are there serious injuries). Therefore, Billie Brown did not breach his duty to act reasonably.[4]

Question Copy

John, age 4, was playing in the playground of his nursery school with his older brother and his friends, who had no school on the day in question. Billie Brown has owned and operated the nursery school for many years. The older children decided to pretend to be knights in a dueling contest and went to the wooded area adjacent to the playground to get some sticks. It did not take long for the game to get out of hand, and John was hit in the eye by a stick thrown by one of the other boys. John's parents sued Billie Brown on behalf of John. What result?

Inferring Negligence—Negligence per se

Question

Tom's Towing (Tom's) had been called to an accident scene on the Green Garden Expressway at 10 p.m. Although the disabled vehicle had been pushed into the median strip, the tow truck was parked so that it was partially in the passing lane as the driver prepared to remove the damaged car. An oncoming car driven by John drove into the back of the tow truck, causing John to break his arm. It was established that the tow truck did not have its emergency lights on at the time

4. Notice that given the absence of any details about the history of such accidents, you could have also argued the other way—a one-time building of a fence, which would not be tremendously expensive, would significantly reduce the likelihood that the sticks would be used on the playground, and everyone knows that playing with sticks can cause someone's eye to be poked—so much so that parents always warn their kids about this. First and foremost, your professor is likely looking for you to show that you understand the basics of the Learned Hand test—that not every act that leads to an injury is a breach, that we compare anticipated harm to the cost of avoiding that harm, and we look at both the probability of the harm and the severity of harm.

of the collision. A state statute required any vehicle stopped on an expressway to use emergency flashers at night. It was also established that John had been properly in the passing lane and had been driving at a steady speed (so you may assume that John was operating the car in a non-negligent manner). Two vehicles had been driving ahead of him until just before the accident. John sues Tom's in negligence. What result?

Notes for Answer

Arguably negligence

Duty is clear—to not endanger others

Standard of care and **breach**—one way to establish the standard of care and breach of that standard is to use negligence per se

Negligence per se:[5]

1. State criminal statute (or sometimes other laws)
   Local ordinances may or may not count
   Licensing requirements often do not count
2. Defines a standard of conduct
   (Doesn't just restate in some way that the defendant must act "with reasonable care")
3. Violation
4. Unexcused
5. Purpose of the statute is related to this situation, judged by two-prong test:
   a. The type of harm to be prevented—emergency flasher requirement almost certainly designed to prevent rear end collisions of this sort
   b. Class of persons intended to be protected—the motoring public

      General argument for court using narrow interpretation or legislative purpose—plaintiff can still prove ad hoc negligence

      General argument for broad interpretation—defendant was already on notice that they should behave in a certain way; civil penalty just adds to the criminal sanction

         Counter—civil penalty could be disproportionately large relative to the criminal penalty
6. Consequence:

   Either automatic (conclusively) negligence, evidence of negligence, or rebuttable presumption of negligence (depending on the jurisdiction)

---

5. Here, elements one through four of negligence per se are clearly met (but in your answer you would want to at least spend a quick sentence on each one).

Here, defendant stopped in the middle of the road without using flasher lights, violating a statute.

There is no apparent excuse (might want to look for one, such as the flashers suddenly not working without negligence by the truck driver)

If the standard of care was breached, discuss factual and **legal cause** (both are fairly straightforward here) and **harm** (which is also clear).

Then, having established the prima facie case for negligence, discuss **defenses**.

Here, you would normally look for contributorily negligent behavior on the part of John, which would bar or reduce recovery, depending on the jurisdiction. But the facts and the assumptions of the question preclude that defense.[6]

Answer

Liability for negligence requires that the plaintiff demonstrate:

1. Duty—owed to the plaintiff
2. Standard of care—normally reasonable person, but with many sub-rules
3. Breach
4. Cause in fact
5. Legal cause
6. Harm
7. With no applicable Defenses

The first issue is whether the tow truck operator's behavior was negligent. The tow truck operator had a duty to not endanger others. The standard of care normally would be reasonable under the circumstances. But one way we can establish the standard of care and breach is by using negligence per se. Depending on the jurisdiction, this either automatically establishes breach, or creates a presumption of breach, or can be used as some evidence of breach.

John would argue that the situation fits the requirements of negligence per se. The plaintiff must demonstrate:

1. A state criminal statute (or sometimes other laws)—a given of the facts
2. That defines a standard of conduct (doesn't just say "must act with reasonable care")—"unlawful to park a motor vehicle on a highway at night without emergency blinkers flashing."
3. A violation—here, no dispute
4. That is unexcused—here, no evidence or claim or by defendant that he couldn't put his blinkers on

---

6. Notice that an excused violation of the statute is not an affirmative defense; it is part of the negligence per se analysis.

5. And purpose of the statute is related to this situation, judged by two-pronged test
   a. The type of harm to be prevented
      The type of harm suffered by the plaintiff was a rear-end collision on the highway, which is the most obvious purpose of the statute.
   b. Class of persons intended to be protected
      The plaintiff was a member of the class the legislature intended to protect with the statute (driver of a car behind a vehicle that doesn't have blinker lights on).
6. Which either establishes breach, a presumption of breach, or evidence of breach (depending on the jurisdiction) — here, the tow truck operator has violated a statute relevant to the accident, and negligence per se is established with the consequences determined by the law of the jurisdiction

Question Copy

Tom's Towing (Tom's) had been called to an accident scene on the Green Garden Expressway at 10 p.m. Although the disabled vehicle had been pushed into the median strip, the tow truck was parked so that it was partially in the passing lane as the driver prepared to remove the damaged car. An oncoming car driven by John drove into the back of the tow truck, causing John to break his arm. It was established that the tow truck did not have its emergency lights on at the time of the collision. A state statute required any vehicle stopped on an expressway to use emergency flashers at night. It was also established that John had been properly in the passing lane and had been driving at a steady speed (so you may assume that John was operating the car in a non-negligent manner). Two vehicles had been driving ahead of him until just before the accident. John sues Tom's in negligence. What result?

Cause in Fact

Remember that in even the simplest of fact situations, cause in fact is still an element, and therefore needs to be addressed. Often this means just a simple application of "but-for" causation. Also remember that the application of "loss of a chance" is most likely in medical situations, where the courts have been most sympathetic to the approach. But unless your professor has indicated otherwise, the loss of a chance approach can be applied by analogy in other settings, even if you aren't given specific percentages to work with (and so long as you make clear that many courts would not use the approach in other than a medical situation). Any time you apply loss of a chance—or for that matter "substantial factor" or any of the common two-cause patterns—there is always the opportunity to discuss policy. Even though factual cause does not involve policy to the extent that legal cause does, in difficult situations the courts may decide whether factual cause is demonstrated in part based on whether the court wants to make it easier for the injured plaintiff to recover.

Question

Sally is skiing on the slopes of a fancy ski resort. She is knocked over by an unskilled skier who does not stop to give her aid. She is on the ground for some time before Lars, a member of the ski patrol, sees her on the ground at the edge of the trail. Rather than immediately giving her aid, he skis back to the chalet where a party is going on. After about an hour he remembers that he had seen Sally, and he goes back to help her. He is able to get her back to the chalet, and she is then rushed to a hospital. Unfortunately she suffered frostbite and the doctors have to amputate her pinky finger. At trial assume that expert evidence shows that she had a 70% chance of losing the finger even if Lars had immediately attempted to rescue her. Also assume that Lars, as a member of the ski patrol, had a duty to assist her. Was the failure of Lars to come to her aid immediately the cause in fact of her losing her finger?

Notes for Answer

Cause in fact

- But-for test

Argument for defendant:

- Here, but-for says no liability
    - She may still have lost the finger without the defendant's negligence
    - Must prove by preponderance of evidence
    - Can't say greater than 50% chance that Lars's negligence caused the injury

Argument for plaintiff:

- Use loss of a chance
    - Not all courts
    - Some only in medical malpractice
    - Lost 30% chance of saving the finger

Policy arguments:

- Ski patrol's duty to aid is to prevent injuries to skiers
- Generally difficult for any nonfeasance plaintiff to recover

Notice first of all that the question asks you to assume there is a duty here. If the call of the question and the assumptions were different, that could be a disputed element.

This is again a reminder that you have to read the call of the question carefully and take into account any assumptions you are given. Here the question only asks about cause in fact. All sorts of other issues might occur to you as you read through the fact pattern, including duty and breach. But that's not what is being asked for. It is a common mistake on an exam to expand the discussion beyond what is asked. Some students find it useful to read the call of the question before reading the rest of the facts.

Answer

Liability for negligence requires that the plaintiff demonstrate:

1. Duty—owed to the plaintiff
2. Standard of care—normally reasonable person, but with many sub-rules
3. Breach
4. Cause in fact
5. Legal cause
6. Harm
7. With no applicable Defenses

Here the other elements are givens or assumed in the question. The issue is whether there is factual cause. The starting point for analysis is but-for causation. We imagine how events would have unfolded without the defendant's negligence. Here but-for is not met. She may still have lost the finger even if the defendant acted non-negligently (rescuing her the first time he saw her). Each element must be proven by a preponderance of evidence. Here we cannot say there is a greater than 50% chance that Lars's inaction caused the injury Sally has suffered.

The argument the plaintiff would make is based on "loss of a chance." Some courts don't accept the argument at all. Many that do accept it allow it only in medical malpractice situations. Here the plaintiff would have to have the court apply the same idea beyond a medical malpractice situation. The plaintiff would argue that Lars's inaction (his negligence) caused her to lose a 30% chance of saving the finger, not that he caused the bad outcome itself. If the court conceives of what was caused as the loss of that 30% chance, and not the final result (losing the finger), the court could find cause in fact is satisfied. There are policy arguments in favor of this. One is the general compensation argument. Without using loss of a chance, it is hard for the plaintiff to recover, even though it is established that Lars breached. It is unlikely that the other possible defendant can be sued for recovery. Also, it is unfair to make it impossible in a situation like this for Sally to recover from Lars when the very reason ski patrol has the duty to aid is to prevent injuries to skiers. In many situations where the defendant failed to act to protect the plaintiff (for example, protecting a customer from a criminal), we will never know whether the same thing would have happened anyway. So even if the courts say there is an exception to the no-duty rule, the defendants would still escape liability because the victim could never establish cause in fact by a preponderance of the evidence.[7]

Question Copy

Sally is skiing on the slopes of a fancy ski resort. She is knocked over by an unskilled skier who does not stop to give her aid. She is on the ground for some time before Lars, a member of the ski patrol, sees her on the ground at the edge of the trail. Rather than immediately giving her aid, he skis back to the chalet where a party is going on. After about an hour he remembers that he had seen Sally and he goes back to help her. He is able to get her back to the chalet, and she is then rushed to a hospital. Unfortunately she suffered frostbite and the doctors have to amputate her pinky finger. At trial assume that expert evidence shows that she had a 70% chance of losing the finger even if Lars had immediately attempted to rescue her. Also assume that Lars, as a member of the ski patrol, had a duty to assist her. Was the failure of Lars to come to her aid immediately the cause in fact of her losing her finger?

Legal (Proximate) Cause

Like the concept of duty, legal or proximate cause puts a limit on a defendant's liability. Both involve discussion of foreseeability, but also involve large doses of policy. For courts that focus on defining duty, the issue is who is a foreseeable plaintiff. For those courts that use legal cause to draw the outer bounds of liability, the analysis centers on what is a foreseeable consequence. Indeed, as we have discussed, in some cases (like the iconic Palsgraf case) one judge may decide the case using duty analysis while another using proximate cause.

Question

The private school track meet was coming up on Saturday. Though Paul was a senior, he had never vaulted at this particular school. The location of the pole vaulting area had been changed because the area normally used was being used for a special trophy presentation and the landing area was closer to the track than usual. The school officials did not mention anything to Paul or his coach. In a practice vault, Paul cleared the bar, landed in the landing area, but his momentum caused him to roll onto the track. He gathered himself, but tripped on the rubbery track, fell, and severely injured his elbow. You may assume that it was a breach to relocate the vaulting area this close to the track. In a suit against the school hosting the track meet by Paul, what result?

---

7. Your professor may have discussed general policy arguments for and against using the loss of a chance idea, so you might want to include them as you write out your own answer.

Notes for Answer

Arguably negligence by the school

Duty—
  To not unreasonably endanger anyone

Standard of Care—
  What a reasonable school would do

Breach—
  Assumed by the facts
    No information to argue against breach, therefore probably not the intended issue in question

Cause in fact—
  But-for test
    He wouldn't have landed on track

Legal or proximate cause—
  Was this an outcome within the foreseeable risk of having the vault too close to the track?

  For the defendant:
    The most foreseeable result from this negligence, and the reasons why we would consider this to be a breach in the first place:
      vaulter could land on the track surface
      maybe also foreseeable that vaulter could be trampled by runners
      winding up on track and tripping is not foreseeable

  For the plaintiff:
    Foreseeable risk—physical injury related to being on the track
      that's what happened
      how it happened doesn't matter if type of injury the same
      thin skull rule—extent of injury doesn't matter
      and here the extent of injury may even be more than expected

Defense
  Paul's possible contributory negligent behavior—applying contributory or comparative negligence
    Few facts here to judge it

Answer

Liability for negligence requires that the plaintiff demonstrate:

1. Duty—owed to the plaintiff
2. Standard of care—normally reasonable person, but with many sub-rules
3. Breach
4. Cause in fact
5. Legal cause
6. Harm
7. With no applicable Defenses

Here, there was a duty on the part of the school to not unreasonably endanger anyone. Certainly this duty would extend to students participating in the track meet, who would be the most foreseeable class of plaintiffs. Breach is assumed by the facts. Cause in fact is met—here, but-for the vaulting pit being so close to the track, Paul would not have landed on the track. Legal (proximate) cause is at issue. The basic test is the risk rule—was this an outcome within the foreseeable risk of having the vault too close to the track? The school would argue the most foreseeable result from its negligence, and the reason why we would consider this to be a breach in the first place, is that a vaulter could injure himself landing on the track surface. It might also be foreseeable that the vaulter could wind up on the track and be trampled by runners on the track. But it is too much of a stretch that the vaulter could wind up on the track and trip because the surface of the track is different from that in the vaulting area. This is not one of the foreseeable risks that makes us consider the location of the vaulting area to be a breach in the first place.

Paul would argue that the foreseeable risk was that the vaulter could get physically injured by being on the track, which would not have happened had the vaulting area been farther away, and that is exactly what happened. Normally courts do not care how exactly the injury happened if it was the type of injury that was foreseeable (here, a physical injury to the elbow). Normally courts hold the defendant responsible for the full extent of the injury even if it is greater than what was foreseeable (thin skull rule). Here, the extent of the injury may not even be greater than what would be expected, and so it is not unfair to hold the school liable. The final element, harm to Paul, is a given of the facts—the injury to his elbow.[8]

---

8. You might then look for any defenses that apply. Arguably Paul is contributorily negligent, though we do not have a lot of facts to make a judgment. But you might want to specify the sort of facts that could establish this defense—"the defendant would argue that Paul should have noticed that the vault would be close to the track, and thus been more careful as he ended his jump."

Question Copy

The private school track meet was coming up on Saturday. Though Paul was a senior, he had never vaulted at this particular school. The location of the pole vaulting area had been changed because the area normally used was being used for a special trophy presentation. and the landing area was closer to the track than usual. The school officials did not mention anything to Paul or his coach. In a practice vault, Paul cleared the bar, landed in the landing area, but his momentum caused him to roll onto the track. He gathered himself, but tripped on the rubbery track, fell, and severely injured his elbow. You may assume that it was a breach to relocate the vaulting area this close to the track, In a suit against the school hosting the track meet by Paul, what result?

Practice Questions

Breach

Question

Kim and Bob Black loved the house the real estate agent Diana had shown them. However, their home inspector said that although there was no evidence of live termites, there was older termite damage in the basement to the main beams supporting the floor structure above. When they expressed their concern to the real estate agent, the agent offered to have the sellers pay for a structural engineer to inspect the house. Diana contacted Steve, a structural engineer and an old friend, and went with him when he looked at the house. She told him that there was a buyer interested in the property. She also told him that the sellers wanted him to inspect three specific areas (the specific areas mentioned in the Blacks' home inspector's report). Steve spent fifteen minutes inspecting only the three areas mentioned. The next day he sent a letter to the real estate agent saying that "he had inspected the basement area" and that, although he found some dry rot, the problems were "structurally insignificant." Diana showed the letter to the Blacks. On the basis of this letter, they bought the house. Shortly after they moved in, they noticed significant structural damage to the house from termites and rot. The Blacks spent in excess of $50,000 repairing the house. In a suit against Steve for negligence, what result?

In most of these questions, we have only discussed one contested or debatable issue, by presenting single-issue fact patterns. However, in an exam setting the call of the question will often be to discuss every element of every tort. This means, unless your professor tells you otherwise, to spend at least a sentence or two on every element, and more time on the element or elements that are most debatable. Here the outline of our answer will focus on whether, if Steve had a duty, he breached it. But since the call of the question is whether there is negligence, you would want to at least address all elements.

If he had duty, did Steve exercise reasonable care in his inspection and report?

Ways to analyze breach

Res ipsa loquitur—not applicable

Negligence per se—not applicable/no statute given

Ad hoc—what is reasonable using common sense

Argument for:

looked at the three areas pointed out to him by the broker
wrote a report that assumed the person reading it had the broker's knowledge of his actions

Argument against:

report said "he had inspected the basement area"—implies all areas
said problems were "structurally insignificant" (clearly wrong if assume all basement investigated)

Own standard—not applicable/none given

Custom—could be applicable if we had evidence of the trade custom

Learned Hand test

Burden—more thorough inspection (cost in time and money)

If burden is less than the expected loss (P x L), then Steve should have taken those steps, and would be found in breach

Probability of bad outcome—a certain percent of defects will go undetected if inspection is limited

Loss/seriousness of bad outcome—some will only cause inconvenience; a certain smaller number will cause significant need for repairs as here

Here is how this answer might begin:

Answer

Liability for negligence requires that the plaintiff demonstrate:

1. Duty—owed to the plaintiff
2. Standard of care—normally reasonable person, but with many sub-rules
3. Breach
4. Cause in fact
5. Legal cause
6. Harm
7. With no applicable Defenses

Steve may have had a duty to the Blacks, even though they did not hire him. Assuming that Steve did have a duty to the Blacks, the next issue is whether he breached that duty. Since he had no professional relationship to them, he did not specifically assume a higher standard of care. So his conduct would be judged by whether he exercised the care that a reasonable person would have exercised....

Question Copy

Kim and Bob Black loved the house the real estate agent Diana had shown them. However, their home inspector said that although there was no evidence of live termites, there was older termite damage in the basement to the main beams supporting the floor structure above. When they expressed their concern to the real estate agent, the agent offered to have the sellers pay for a structural engineer to inspect the house. Diana contacted Steve, a structural engineer and an old friend, and went with him when he looked at the house. She told him that there was a buyer interested in the property. She also told him that the sellers wanted him to inspect three specific areas (the specific areas mentioned in the Blacks' home inspector's report). Steve spent fifteen minutes inspecting only the three areas mentioned. The next day he sent a letter to the real estate agent saying that "he had inspected the basement area" and that, although he found some dry rot, the problems were "structurally insignificant." Diana showed the letter to the Blacks. On the basis of this letter, they bought the house. Shortly after they moved in, they noticed significant structural damage to the house from termites and rot. The Blacks spent in excess of $50,000 repairing the house. In a suit against Steve for negligence, what result?

Inferring Breach—Res Ipsa Loquitur

Although usually the evidence of breach is based on knowledge of what happened, with the debate centering on whether what the defendant did was a breach of the applicable standard of care, res ipsa loquitur is an approach to finding negligence when there is no direct evidence of what the defendant did.

Question

Pauline, a driver for the Apex Transport Company, backed up her truck at the loading dock of Mann Auto Parts (Mann) to pick up batteries for a customer. The center door was a standard overhead garage door operating on tracks. It was open so Pauline did not touch, much less operate the door. While she was standing in the doorway loading the batteries into her truck, the door rolled down and struck Pauline on the head. She fell to the floor. There was no one else nearby. After she got up she noticed wood debris on the floor a few feet away. She was sure it had not been there before. There also was a spring mechanism dangling to one side of the door.

Employees of Mann Auto Parts unlocked the doors each morning and locked them each evening. As a tenant, Mann was responsible for the leased premises. The doors had not been inspected by Mann for at least two years before the accident. No one other than Mann employees had permission to open the doors. In a suit by Pauline against Mann for negligence, what result?

Notes for Answer

Arguably negligent behavior

Duty—general duty to not endanger others

Standard of Care—reasonable under the circumstances

Breach—Res Ipsa Loquitur (no direct evidence)

1. This is not the type of injury that normally occurs in the absence of negligence OR the injury was more likely than not the result of negligence (two different ways of stating the same thing)

   Argument for:
   open door fell
   debris and dangling mechanism
   no other person near

   Argument against:
   debris could have been result of falling door, not cause
   others could have left the door partially open earlier

2. Defendant was in sole control (traditional rule—narrow)

   OR, taking into account any other causes (including the plaintiff), it was more likely than not the defendant's negligence (modern rule—broader)

   Ruling out other third party causes

   Argument for:
   doors unlocked by employees
   doors operated by others, but only with Mann's knowledge

   Argument against:
   door operated by others

   Ruling out the plaintiff's conduct

   Pauline didn't touch the door
   no evidence that standing under the door loading helped cause it to close on her

3. The negligence was within the scope of the defendant's duty to the plaintiff

Cause in fact—but-for causation: but for Mann negligently dealing with the door, Pauline would not have been injured

Legal or proximate cause— risk rule clearly satisfied

If the door is negligently maintained, it is foreseeable that it will fall and injure someone, which is exactly what happened

Harm—a given that Pauline was injured

Question Copy

Pauline, a driver for the Apex Transport Company, backed up her truck at the loading dock of Mann Auto Parts (Mann) to pick up batteries for a customer. The center door was a standard overhead garage door operating on tracks. It was open so Pauline did not touch, much less operate the door. While she was standing in the doorway loading the batteries into her truck, the door rolled down and struck Pauline on the head. She fell to the floor. There was no one else nearby. After she got up she noticed wood debris on the floor a few feet away. She was sure it had not been there before. There also was a spring mechanism dangling to one side of the door.

Employees of Mann Auto Parts unlocked the doors each morning and locked them each evening. As a tenant, Mann was responsible for the leased premises. The doors had not been inspected by Mann for at least two years before the accident. No one other than Mann employees had permission to open the doors. In a suit by Pauline against Mann for negligence, what result?

Legal (Proximate) Cause

Question

Peter was a track star at Elite Country Day School, a private high school. He had just finished his practice run on the indoor track in preparation for a meet the following weekend. He climbed almost six feet up on a ladder near the track to sit on a platform-like step to see the action better. Although the school had a policy forbidding anyone but the maintenance personnel from climbing the ladder, there was no sign. A student supervisor who saw Peter come out of the gym didn't keep Peter off the ladder, and there were no faculty or administration supervisors anywhere near the ladder. When Peter saw his friend Paul fall on the track after his pole vaulting run, Peter jumped off the ladder to help. His thumb caught in an unusually tight intersecting metal joint of the ladder and severe injury was done to the tendon. In a suit by Peter against the school, what result?

Notes for Answer

Arguably negligence

Duty—

Misfeasance? Did school endanger?
Or nonfeasance? Arguably duty to protect
Possibly landowner's liability—duty based on Peter's status

Standard of Care—

What a reasonable school should do
Or a more clearly court-defined standard if court finds a specific duty to protect
Or a definition of the standard based on Peter's status

Breach—

Little information to argue about the breach, therefore probably not the most contested issue

Possible acts of breach:

The main one is failing to keep Peter off the ladder
Not enough supervisors around/no faculty or administration
Negligent training of the student supervisors
Failure to have sign on ladder
Student supervisors didn't tell Peter to get off ladder

Also, the ladder itself
Failure to inspect and replace dangerous joint

Ways to think about and analyze breach:

Ad hoc— general, common sense argument about what is reasonable

Negligence per se— no statute given; hard to imagine one that applies

Res ipsa loquitur— we know what happened, therefore inapplicable

Custom— hard to apply this (maybe customary to use a certain kind of ladder or joint, but few facts given)

Own standard— school had policy against people on ladder
Can't use defendant's own standard to deviate from "reasonableness" standard
But can be used as some evidence of negligence

Learned Hand Test—compare burden (cost) to probability and loss/seriousness of anticipated injury (benefit)

Did cost of avoiding accident exceed foreseeable cost of harm? If not, breach

Cause in fact—

But for Peter being allowed to be on the ladder, no injury to him

Legal (proximate) cause—

For defendant:

Narrow definition of the foreseeable risk—someone will fall from the ladder

For plaintiff:

Broader definition that is arguably based on foresight and not hindsight—someone will be physically injured by being on the ladder
Normally the way it which injury happens doesn't matter

Counter by defendant:

This was a totally different type of injury that had nothing to do with failing to stop someone from being at the top of a six-foot ladder

Harm—

Peter's injury a given

No applicable Defenses

Additional rule—if any of the employees or people under Elite's supervision were liable for negligence, Elite would likely be liable using *respondeat superior.*

There are lots of issues in this short problem, aren't there? Now try writing out your answer to some or all of them.

Question Copy

Peter was a track star at Elite Country Day School, a private high school. He had just finished his practice run on the indoor track in preparation for a meet the following weekend. He climbed almost six feet up on a ladder near the track to sit on a platform-like step to see the action better. Although the school had a policy forbidding anyone but the maintenance personnel from climbing the ladder, there was no sign. A student supervisor who saw Peter come out of the gym didn't keep Peter off the ladder, and there were no faculty or administration supervisors anywhere near the ladder. When Peter saw his friend Paul fall on the track after his pole vaulting run, Peter jumped off the ladder to help. His thumb caught in an unusually tight intersecting metal joint of the ladder and severe injury was done to the tendon. In a suit by Peter against the school, what result?

Multiple Parties

Here is the skiing fact pattern we used at the beginning of this chapter. This will give you a chance to practice writing multi-party answers.

Question

Janet and Bill were just married. They decided to go on their honeymoon to Snow Woods, one of the best ski resorts in the country. Janet was an expert skier, but Bill had only started skiing when he met Janet two years before. When they bought their lift tickets, the ticket seller said, "Be glad you weren't here yesterday. Man, was it crowded. We had our busiest day this season." Janet agreed to ski with Bill on the intermediate level trails in the morning and then leave him to go to the advanced level trails in the afternoon. Although there hadn't been much snow, they knew Snow Woods had great snowmaking equipment. The first run went well, so they decided to try the next most difficult intermediate trail, the very popular Owl View Trail.

As they approached the middle of the run, Bill suddenly was hit from behind by a novice skier for whom this trail was obviously beyond his capabilities. The skier continued on his way. Bill went sprawling. He screamed in pain as he tried to get up. Janet had been skiing behind Bill to help him improve his form. She immediately started towards Bill.

She saw someone they had met the night before at dinner skiing toward them. He was a physician with whom they had spent the evening discussing health care reform. She felt relief, but only momentarily. The physician looked right at Bill and then skied away. Janet arrived at Bill's side when two teenage boys stopped, took off their parkas and made a sling to carry Bill down the mountain. They didn't do a good job of it, and he slipped out of the sling further damaging his foot. What torts?

Answer

Liability for negligence requires that the plaintiff demonstrate:

1. Duty—owed to the plaintiff
2. Standard of care—normally reasonable person, but with many sub-rules
3. Breach
4. Cause in fact
5. Legal cause
6. Harm
7. With no applicable Defenses

Bill v. Novice Skier (for failing to come to Bill's aid)

Usually someone cannot be liable in negligence for failure to protect or come to the aid of a person exposed to danger by someone or something else. The law imposes no duty to act. However, there are exceptions. Here, ...

Bill v. Snow Woods Resort

Bill v. Teenagers

Bill v. Physician

Bill v. Novice Skier (for endangering Bill by being on the wrong slope)

You will notice that the novice skier is listed in two separate sections of the answer. Skiing on the wrong slope allows for an argument that the novice skier endangered another person—misfeasance. The novice skier also arguably had a duty to come to Bill's aid, whether negligent or not—a nonfeasance exception. It is important to look for more than one tort or argument for a given party. It is also important to look for torts by "phantom parties"—parties who are not given names (the "novice skier") or parties that seem to be part of the background whose actions are not the focus of the fact pattern (the ski resort).

Also notice that you could put these parties in different order. One way to answer the question is to list each party who may have had a duty to aid or protect Bill, and then to look for any party who endangered him (the novice skier). Another way to organize your answer would be by parties—you would address both of the theories of recovery against the novice skier, and then move on. There is no right or wrong way to organize multi-party questions. The key is to make sure you address every possible party combination and tort. But if, as here, several claims are similar (the various parties who all failed to aid or rescue) you may want to put those claims one after the other in your answer so you can save time by stating the governing rules once (here, the rule covering duty in a nonfeasance situation, along with exceptions).

Question Copy

Janet and Bill were just married. They decided to go on their honeymoon to Snow Woods, one of the best ski resorts in the country. Janet was an expert skier, but Bill had only started skiing when he met Janet two years before. When they bought their lift tickets, the ticket seller said, "Be glad you weren't here yesterday. Man, was it crowded. We had our busiest day this season." Janet agreed to ski with Bill on the intermediate level trails in the morning and then leave him to go to the advanced level trails in the afternoon. Although there hadn't been much snow, they knew Snow Woods had great snowmaking equipment. The first run went well, so they decided to try the next most difficult intermediate trail, the very popular Owl View Trail.

As they approached the middle of the run, Bill suddenly was hit from behind by a novice skier for whom this trail was obviously beyond his capabilities. The skier continued on his way. Bill went sprawling. He screamed in pain as he tried to get up. Janet had been skiing behind Bill to help him improve his form. She immediately started towards Bill.

She saw someone they had met the night before at dinner skiing toward them. He was a physician with whom they had spent the evening discussing health care reform. She felt relief, but only momentarily. The physician looked right at Bill and then skied away. Janet arrived at Bill's side when two teenage boys stopped, took off their parkas and made a sling to carry Bill down the mountain. They didn't do a good job of it, and he slipped out of the sling further damaging his foot. What torts?

Chapter 4

Strict Liability and Products Liability

Analysis Hints

One way to connect negligence to strict liability is to understand that intentional tort, negligence, and strict liability can be viewed as a continuum from the greatest amount of fault to the least. The following rule is almost the same as the negligence rule we presented earlier, but the elements of duty and standard of care have now been made into an absolute duty to prevent injury based merely on the fact that the defendant acted (regardless of how careful the defendant was).

Rule: To prevail on a claim of strict liability, plaintiff must show that defendant:

1. engaged in an **Abnormally Dangerous Activity**
2. that was the **Cause in Fact**
3. and the **Legal Cause**
4. of **Harm** to the plaintiff

You will probably study two major areas of strict liability—animals and abnormally dangerous activities. Many professors and casebooks emphasize the historical origins of this theory of recovery from the *Rylands v. Fletcher* case. Some professors and casebooks include products liability under the umbrella of strict liability; others treat it as a separate section of the course entirely. Things can get a bit confusing, because one category of products liability (manufacturing defect) reflects true strict liability. The other categories—design defects and warning defects—have aspects of strict liability, but most professors and most courts treat these categories as in reality "stricter liability" (stricter than negligence), but not true strict liability. And the term products liability can have two meanings (similar to what we saw with the word negligence). Products liability can refer to purely torts-based recovery for various types of defects (manufacturing, design, and warning). It can also refer to various theories, all of which can be used when someone gets injured from the use of a product—express warranty, implied warranty of merchantability, and misrepresentation. These theories mostly originated in contract law, but have aspects of tort law as well.

We will first address "true" strict liability (animals and abnormally dangerous activities) and then address the general category of products liability (focusing on the tort theory of recovery commonly called "products liability"). For both of these topics, but especially for products liability, your professor may approach the subject from any number of philosophical points of view. It is important to identify the approach used in your class and to be prepared to add your professor's "take" on the subject to the doctrinally oriented answers you will find in this chapter.

For true strict liability—animals and abnormally dangerous activity—your professor may go into great detail in terms of the rules. Or your class may just focus on the basics, and take as a given that certain activities—blasting with dynamite and shipment of hazardous waste, to give two examples—are clearly abnormally dangerous. So a more detailed version of the "abnormally dangerous" part of your outline might include factors from the Restatement as to what is or isn't abnormally dangerous, policy arguments about non-reciprocal risk, etc. But the essential elements are an abnormally dangerous activity that caused harm to the plaintiff of the sort that was within the risk that makes this activity abnormally dangerous. Because the liability is "strict," the care taken by the defendant does not matter—the defendant must bear the cost even if he acted reasonably.

For true strict liability, categorizing the activity as "abnormally dangerous" substitutes for the duty, standard of care, and breach elements (as shown by the initial rule presented at the beginning of this chapter). In such cases, the defendant has a duty to not endanger others by engaging in the activity. The standard of care and the definition of breach become "strict" rather than based on reasonableness—if defendant acted causing injury, they are liable. But this means that cause in fact and legal (proximate) cause must still be demonstrated. For example, if toxic waste is spilled by a truck hauling it, the plaintiff must still prove that the illness they complain of was caused by exposure to the toxic waste, and not some other cause. Similarly, if the plaintiff slips on the spill and breaks an arm, there would be no strict liability due to the rules of legal cause. Do you see why? Here we would have a case where the injury (a broken arm) is not within the scope of the risk. Stated another way, the risk of someone breaking an arm by slipping on spilled hazardous waste is not why we consider this activity to be abnormally dangerous in the first place. The foreseeable risk that caused us to label this abnormally dangerous, and therefore to impose strict liability, is the risk of the kind of illness or disease that would result from exposure to the toxic waste.

For products liability in torts, remember—there is a difference between a manufacturing defect and a design defect. In the real world, if we know all the facts, a given situation is likely to be one or the other but not both. The key distinction is this—does this unit deviate from the others (like the one Coca-Cola bottle that is more prone to explode)? If so, it's a manufacturing defect. If all the units are the same, with the same alleged defect (for example, an automobile that didn't have side airbags), it's a design defect.

On an exam your professor may want you to efficiently assess both. So make sure you aren't jumping over one possible defect by making certain assumptions that aren't clearly made in the fact pattern. To use a real-world example, think about the allegations against Toyota that some of their cars had "sudden acceleration" that caused injuries. As of this writing we don't know whether some or all of these accidents were caused by driver error or other factors not attributable to the car itself. But assuming they were not, it is possible that a few individual cars had a problem not shared with others of the same model. For example, despite the best manufacturing techniques available, slight deviations in the physical characteristics of the accelerator linkage may cause a few cars to "stick" more than others. This might be considered a manufacturing defect (akin to the exploding Coca-Cola bottle in classic cases; a bottle which deviated slightly from others despite the manufacturer's best efforts). It is also possible that there is something about the design of the electronic system related to the fuel injection that causes these accidents (a design defect; all of the cars have the same system, which happens to be a bad design). On a law school exam you may think the professor has set up a fact pattern to test your knowledge of the rules governing design defects—the rules governing design defects are more complicated and therefore more likely to be tested. But you need to make sure that it is clear that this unit was identical to all the others. If that is not a given of the facts, you need to think about whether a manufacturing defect could explain the accident. And of course, if it is not absolutely clear, you always want to argue in the alternative.

Draft Outline

Wild Animals

Rule: Strict liability applies when an animal being kept by the defendant:

1. Had a **Propensity for Dangerous Behavior** that was known or should have been known by the defendant
2. The animal was the **Cause** of
3. **Harm** to the plaintiff
4. Of the type that was **Within the Risk** of that animal's dangerousness
   The care taken by the defendant does not matter—the defendant must bear the cost (including costs imposed on the plaintiff) even if the defendant acted reasonably

Abnormally Dangerous Activity

Rule: Strict liability applies when the defendant:

1. Engaged in an **Abnormally Dangerous Activity**
2. That was the **Cause** of
3. **Harm** to the plaintiff
4. Of the type that was **Within the Risk** that makes this activity abnormally dangerous
   The care taken by the defendant does not matter—the defendant must bear the cost (including costs imposed on the plaintiff) even if the defendant acted reasonably

Your professor may want to test your ability to argue that a certain activity should or should not trigger strict liability. If so, your casebook reading may include the relevant section of the Restatement with the factors courts use. Or the fact pattern your professor gives you may use a prototypical example—dynamite blasting or transport of hazardous waste, for example—to test other aspects of the strict liability rules (for example, cause in fact or legal cause, or perhaps a more policy-oriented question where the classification of the activity as abnormally dangerous is not at issue).

As discussed earlier, products liability in torts is not true strict liability (except for manufacturing defects). With that in mind, here is the beginning of a sample outline for products liability.

Draft Outline: Products Liability

Theories for recovery for injury by products other than the theory of "products liability" in torts—

Express warranty
Implied warranty
Misrepresentation
Negligence[1]

Products liability (as a separate theory of tort recovery):

1. **Defective product**

   Three types:

   A. Manufacturing defect
      True strict liability

   B. Design defect
      Restatement Second test—"consumer expectation" test
         Also used for food (regardless of whether the jurisdiction uses the "consumer expectation" test or the "risk-utility" test for other products)
      Restatement Third test—"risk-utility analysis"
         First, do cost-benefit analysis of the anticipated risks of the current design compared with the cost of avoiding them (Learned Hand test—as with a negligence case)
         Then, plaintiff must also show there was a "reasonable alternative design"
         1. An alternative design
         2. Economically feasible
         3. Technologically feasible
         4. The alternative would have reduced the probability of this type of accident
         5. The alternative would not have caused other problems or dangers that outweigh the advantage of reducing this danger

   C. Warning defect
      Adequate warning[2]
      1. Conspicuous—available to or noticeable by user
      2. Informs user that there are risks
      3. Conveys nature and severity or the risk
      4. Explains how to use safely

---

1. Some professors will spend a lot of time on the theories listed above, comparing and contrasting them to products liability in tort. Others will gloss over them, perhaps giving some historical context but not requiring you to know them for the exam.

2. These factors are from Ronald Eades, *Mastering Products Liability* (Carolina Academic Press, 2008).

2. **Cause in Fact**
3. **Legal (Proximate) Cause**
4. **Harm**
5. With no applicable **Defenses**

Defenses:

Under **contributory negligence**—traditionally does NOT bar recovery in products liability

Rationale—focus is on the product, not the defendant's behavior

Defendant shouldn't get off the hook by the happenstance of who was injured by a defective product

Under **comparative negligence**—modern view DOES reduce recovery

Compares "responsibility" of plaintiff with that of defendant

Common counterarguments made by defendant to negate finding that the product is defective (not true affirmative defenses):

Unavoidably dangerous products—including drugs

Obviously dangerous—"product as its own warning"

Learned intermediary rule

Product misuse—if the product was dangerous only if unforeseeably misused by the plaintiff, it was not defective in the first place

Other rules applicable to products liability:

a. Once establishing that there is a defect, it must be shown that the defect existed at the time it left defendant's control
b. Defendant can be anyone in the chain of distribution who is regularly in the business: manufacturer, distributor, or retailer of new cars, or a used-car dealer (but not your neighbor selling her used car). This is different than negligence, where any defendant must have had a clear duty to the plaintiff and must have breached that duty (for example, by failing to inspect the product).

Other ways products liability is "more strict" than negligence:

a. Even if court uses risk-utility test from the Third Restatement (which seems to resemble negligence)—shift burden to defendant to disprove defect (minority view)
b. Anyone in chain of distribution is potential defendant (in almost all courts, unless jurisdiction has a "sealed container" rule that applies)
c. Focus on the product rather than defendant's behavior (common rhetoric by court)

Rule:

1. A **Defective Product**[3] (manufacturing, design or warning defect)
2. Was the **Cause in Fact**
3. And **Legal Cause** of
4. Plaintiff's **Harm**
5. **Defenses**
   Some courts do not apply the usual rules of contributory or comparative negligence to products liability cases

The product was defective at the time it left the defendant's control (did not undergo significant change before reaching the consumer)

The defendant was in the chain of distribution and was in the business of supplying the product

Sample Questions

Abnormally Dangerous Activity

Question

Transcontinental Oil owns a pipeline which carries oil from the north of Canada to the United States. The pipeline was constructed in conformance with all industry guidelines, and there were no problems with its operation for four years. The pipeline goes through many forested and farming areas. In a remote area of Montana one of the welded seams of the pipeline broke, spilling oil. The oil got into a pond used to irrigate crops, causing damage to Frank's pond and to his crops before the leak was detected. In a suit by Frank against Transcontinental Oil, what result?

---

3. As was the case with an abnormally dangerous activity in true strict liability, defectiveness of the product substitutes for the duty, standard, and breach steps of analysis.

Notice that in addition to the elements that parallel the negligence elements ("defective product" as substitute for duty, standard, and breach; cause in fact; legal cause; injury), there are additional rules that apply to products liability, and therefore additional steps you must address in your analysis. And also notice that for products liability there are several different counterarguments that look like defenses, and are sometimes referred to as such by courts, but are really arguments that go to whether the product was "defective" as part of the prima facie case.

Notes for Answer

Strict liability for damage caused by an abnormally dangerous activity requires:

1. Abnormally dangerous activity
   Based on various factors under the Restatement *or* historically accepted categories (depending on your professor's approach)
2. That causes harm
3. The harm is within the risk that makes this an abnormally dangerous activity (legal cause)
   The care taken by the defendant is irrelevant; defendant must bear the cost even if they acted reasonably. (This is not really a separate element—a policy explanation and a reminder that fault does not play a role.)
4. With no applicable defenses (for true strict liability contributory negligence traditionally didn't apply; a court may or may not reduce recovery using comparative fault/responsibility)

Answer

For the plaintiff to recover using a strict liability theory, she must show the defendant engaged in an abnormally dangerous activity, the activity of the defendant caused harm (regardless of how much care was taken), and the harm is within the risk that makes this an abnormally dangerous activity. Here, operating an oil pipeline is an activity which is traditionally considered an abnormally dangerous activity, and the leak in the pipeline clearly caused the harm (a given of the problem). Even though Transcontinental Oil lived up to industry guidelines, that is irrelevant under strict liability—the defendant must bear the cost of this activity rather than the plaintiff. The pipeline poses a non-reciprocal risk to the pond and crops.[4]

Question Copy

Transcontinental Oil owns a pipeline which carries oil from the north of Canada to the United States. The pipeline was constructed in conformance with all industry guidelines, and there were no problems with its operation for four years. The pipeline goes through many forested and farming areas. In a remote area of Montana one of the welded seams of the pipeline broke, spilling oil. The oil got into a pond used to irrigate crops, causing damage to Frank's pond and to his crops before the leak was detected. In a suit by Frank against Transcontinental Oil, what result?

---

4. Depending on your professor, you might want to go into greater depth explaining why this is considered an abnormally dangerous activity or the policy reasons why the defendant rather than the plaintiff should bear the cost of this activity, which benefits society but creates risk.

Manufacturing Defect

Question

Black Motor Company manufactured an automobile that it sold to Cain Cars, a retail dealer, which in turn sold it to Kevin. Kevin bought the car because it was a model that had several years of high rankings by several consumer groups. He was a traveling salesman who depended upon the reliable performance of his car. On his first use of his new car, Kevin drove from his suburban home into the city to meet his fiancée, Melinda, for dinner. There were traffic lights at each intersection so he was not able to go very fast. Approaching one intersection he saw the traffic light facing him turn from green to yellow. He thought he could get across the intersection before the light turned red so he sped up. However, as he got closer he realized that he couldn't make it through the intersection and applied the brakes. The brakes failed. Kevin steered sharply to the right to avoid the cars that were by now crossing in front of him. The car went onto the sidewalk where fortunately the car stopped without hitting anyone or anything. However, Kevin suffered severe whiplash and was in constant pain for months thereafter. What are the rights and liabilities of the parties?

Notes for Answer

Rule: A defective product—manufacturing, design, or warning **Defect**

Was the **Cause in Fact**

And **Legal Cause** of

Plaintiff's **Harm**

Defenses

The product was defective at the time it left the defendant's control (did not undergo significant change before reaching the consumer)

The defendant was in the chain of distribution and was in the business of supplying the product

Kevin v. Black Motor Company

Defective product—brakes failed soon after purchase

When left defendant's control—no change before getting to consumer since no evidence Cain Cars touched the brakes

Cause in fact and legal cause satisfied—foreseeable person injured and foreseeable outcome—Kevin bought the car; Kevin suffered physical injury

Injury to plaintiff—obviously

Defenses—none apparent

Commercial supplier—Black Motor Company

Kevin v. Cain Cars

(Same analysis as above as to the defect)

Cain is a commercial supplier of the item; products liability allows suit against anyone in the chain of distribution

It does not matter whether Cain had a duty to inspect (they probably did not have such a duty) nor whether Cain in fact inspected (this would matter if Cain were a defendant in a negligence action, but not under a products liability theory). If Cain is successfully sued, it may seek indemnification from Black, the party that is ultimately responsible, but that dispute is between Black and Cain. Kevin can sue either or both.

Answer

Kevin v. Black Motor Company

Black Motor Company may be liable under a products liability theory. There must be a defective product. Here, there is no evidence that this is a design defect. The car has gotten good recommendations from consumer groups for years. A design defect would have been discovered by the time Kevin bought this particular car. It is therefore likely that the brake failure was a manufacturing defect—this one unit did not perform as others did. If so, no matter how much care was taken by the manufacturer, the product is still considered defective; it is not a question of negligence. Since there is no evidence that the product underwent significant changes before reaching Kevin, it seems clear that the brakes were defective when the car left Black's control.[5]

In a suit based on products liability, the injured person can sue anyone in the chain of distribution who was in the business of supplying the product. That obviously applies to the manufacturer.[6]

Kevin v. Cain Cars

The same analysis applies to defining the product as defective for this defendant as for Black. Under a negligence theory, the retailer (Cain) might have no duty to inspect or know about a potential problem, and might not be liable. But under a products liability theory, any entity in the commercial business of putting the car on the market, including the retailer, Cain Cars, is liable if the product is defective and the other elements are met. Cain might, if found liable, be able to seek

---

5. Next you would discuss cause in fact and legal cause, both of which are pretty clearly satisfied.

6. Next you would discuss any potential defenses.

indemnification from Black, but Cain is jointly and severally liable (or severally, if that is the rule in this jurisdiction.)[7]

Question Copy

Black Motor Company manufactured an automobile that it sold to Cain Cars, a retail dealer, which in turn sold it to Kevin. Kevin bought the car because it was a model that had several years of high rankings by several consumer groups. He was a traveling salesman who depended upon the reliable performance of his car. On his first use of his new car, Kevin drove from his suburban home into the city to meet his fiancée, Melinda, for dinner. There were traffic lights at each intersection so he was not able to go very fast. Approaching one intersection he saw the traffic light facing him turn from green to yellow. He thought he could get across the intersection before the light turned red so he sped up. However, as he got closer he realized that he couldn't make it through the intersection and applied the brakes. The brakes failed. Kevin steered sharply to the right to avoid the cars that were by now crossing in front of him. The car went onto the sidewalk where fortunately the car stopped without hitting anyone or anything. However, Kevin suffered severe whiplash and was in constant pain for months thereafter. What are the rights and liabilities of the parties?

Design Defect

Question

Bill was hired in October by the Firehouse Condominiums as building superintendent. For several months he kept busy learning the quirks of the renovated building and developing a maintenance routine. He was just getting to the point where he felt that he had the property under control when the first snowstorm struck unexpectedly at noon. He had seen an Advance snow thrower in the maintenance shed and realized that it was a lightweight model, designed to remove snow only a few inches deep. He personally owned a similar lightweight machine of a different make that he used at his home. There was no Advance instruction booklet in the maintenance shed and no instructions on the machine itself.

He filled the tank with fuel, took the snow thrower outside, and began work. After a few minutes he realized that the discharge chute needed to be unclogged. He let go of the handle and reached into the chute. His hand was severely cut because the machine did not have what is called a "dead man's" control—a device which automatically stops the rotation of the auger when the operator lets go of

7. Next you would discuss any potential defenses.

the handle. His own snow thrower had such a device, as did all other snow throwers on the market. The instruction booklet for this particular model warned against clearing the discharge chute of snow with the machine running. In a suit by Bill against Advance, what result (using the consumer expectation test)?

Notes for Answer

Defective product unreasonably dangerous

Consumer expectation test:

General expectation — that snow blower be safe for average user

All other snow throwers have the dead man control — this makes expectation more reasonable and would be the basis for such expectation

Consumer is not unrealistically "over-expecting" safety

Counter—it has lots of moving parts; a normal consumer might expect some danger

Adequate warning

1. Conspicuous—available to or noticeable by user
2. Informs user that there are risks
3. Conveys nature and severity or the risk
4. Explains how to use safely

Arguments for:

Warning in instruction booklet given to purchaser

The product is obviously dangerous — it is "its own warning"

Arguments against:

Warnings must reach all foreseeable users

Employee or second owner foreseeable users, can't assume will get instruction booklet

Warning must be sufficiently urgent and prominent — for this kind of danger the warning should have been on the machine

Answer

The plaintiff, to recover using a products liability theory, must demonstrate:

1. A defective product—manufacturing, design or warning **Defect**
2. was the **Cause in Fact**
3. and **Legal Cause** of
4. plaintiff's **Harm**
5. with no applicable **Defenses**

The product was defective at the time it left the defendant's control (did not undergo significant change before reaching the consumer).

The defendant was in the chain of distribution (was in the business of supplying the product).

Here—applying the consumer expectation test—plaintiff would argue that this product was unsafe to an extent beyond which would be contemplated by the ordinary consumer. Since all other available snow throwers (including Bill's own) were equipped with a dead man's control, it would be reasonable for the ordinary consumer to expect that safety level. The fact that the Advance model did not have it would make for a strong argument that the dangerous condition here would not be expected by the ordinary consumer.

Advance as a commercial supplier has sold the product, making it one of several potential defendants. This product was designed without the safety device, meaning it was defective when it left the defendant's control, and there is no evidence that the product underwent any significant changes before reaching the consumer. The user of the product—someone who might be foreseeably endangered by the product—was injured.

A commercial supplier of a product is strictly liable for any injury the product causes if it is a defective product unreasonably dangerous. One test used by courts to determine whether a product is unreasonably dangerous is the consumer expectation test. A product is unreasonably dangerous if it is more dangerous than would be apparent to an ordinary consumer using the product. Manufacturers producing dangerous products may be found not to be liable if they have provided an adequate warning of the danger. Although there may have been adequate warnings in the instruction booklet, to avoid liability the defendant must take steps to ensure that the warnings reach foreseeable users. In the case of a snow thrower, it is certainly reasonable to assume that someone other than the original purchaser might be using it. If Advance failed to provide the dead man's control at a time when it was standard on every other snow thrower, this might make the product defective. But a warning might reduce the risk to the point where the product would no longer be considered defective (though if the danger is too great, a warning will not exonerate the defendant). Here the plaintiff could have been made aware of this danger by putting a warning label on the machine itself. Here there was no warning on the machine. Therefore, Advance did not give adequate warning.

Since Advance produced a dangerous machine and sold it without adequate warning to the consumer, it would be liable to Bill.

Question Copy

Bill was hired in October by the Firehouse Condominiums as building superintendent. For several months he kept busy learning the quirks of the renovated building and developing a maintenance routine. He was just getting to the point where he felt that he had the property under control when the first snowstorm struck unexpectedly at noon. He had seen an Advance snow thrower in the maintenance shed and realized that it was a light-weight model, designed to remove snow only a few inches deep. He personally owned a similar small machine of a different make that he used at his home. There was no Advance instruction booklet in the maintenance shed and no instructions on the machine itself.

He filled the tank with fuel, took the snow thrower outside, and began work. After a few minutes he realized that the discharge chute needed to be unclogged of snow. He let go of the handle and reached into the chute. His hand was severely cut because the machine did not have what is called a "dead man's" control, a device which automatically stops the rotation of the auger when the operator lets go of the handle. His own snow thrower had such a device, as did all other snow throwers on the market. The instruction booklet for this particular model warned against clearing the discharge chute of snow with the machine running. In a suit by Bill against Advance, what result?

Practice Question

Question

Paula had been working at the Beta Plastics Company (Beta) assembly line all day and was looking forward to an evening of bowling. Today's work, making plastic hockey pucks, required that she operate the press twice for each puck. Often the plastic stuck to the top die, and she had to peel the plastic free. Once, as she reached up to free the plastic from the die, she inadvertently hit the activator foot pedal, and the press crushed her hand.

The machine was sold to Beta by Careful Technologies (Careful) fifteen years earlier when there were no industry standards for any safety features. Although the machine Paula was working on had no safety features, Careful had design modifications and safety devices available at the time which would have prevented Paula's injury. Five years after Beta bought the machine, Careful sent information about the safety devices to Beta and also sent accident-preventing warning labels to be affixed to the machine. Identical information was sent each of the next four years. Beta never responded to the letters, nor did it install any of the safety devices or affix the warning labels. Paula sues Careful. What result?

Notes for Answer

The plaintiff, to recover using a products liability theory must demonstrate:

1. A defective product—manufacturing, design or warning **Defect**
2. was the **Cause in Fact**
3. and **Legal Cause** of
4. plaintiff's **Harm**
5. with no applicable **Defenses**

the product was defective at the time it left the defendant's control (did not undergo significant change before reaching the consumer)

the defendant was in the chain of distribution (was in the business of supplying the product)

Design defect

Restatement Second—consumer expectation test

Would a normal consumer/user expect the machine to be safe?

Or would consumers/users know that such machines are not perfectly safe?

Here, the consumer expectation test seems to help the defendant (whereas it often helps the plaintiff)

Restatement Third—risk/utility test, with reasonable alternative design

1. Risk/utility balance:

   High probability of injury, some of which could be severe

   Burden/cost to avoid would be redesigning the safety interlock—unknown cost—probably not trivial, but probably less than the cost of the foreseeable bad outcomes

2. Reasonable alternative design:

   Alternative—safety device modifications available

   Economically feasible—cost not given; probably not trivial but no evidence that it would be prohibitive; but it might slow down process, which is a form of cost

   Technologically feasible—the alternatives exist

Alternative would reduce probability of this type of injury—yes

Alternative would not cause other problems — no evidence that it would

Counter — maybe the way safety device works causes operator to become fatigued more quickly or to be in a more dangerous position

Arguments against liability:

1. Superseding cause—Beta (didn't install devices)
2. Passage of time — possible statute of repose issue
3. Paula misused the machine

Contributory negligence—some jurisdictions disregard

Misuse—arguably no defect if only dangerous with misuse;
counter — misuse was foreseeable

Adequacy of warning

Conspicuous/available to or noticeable by user

Given to Beta, not to ultimate user (possible application of learned intermediary rule or liability by Beta); if posted on machine, it would meet the test

Informs user that there are risks

Not clear from facts what the warning labels said

Conveys nature and severity or the risk

Not clear from facts what the warning labels said

Explains how to use safely

Not clear from facts

No duty to remedy a past defect

Jurisdictions differ

Careful *did* engage in post-sale remedy — should this even be admissible?

If Careful does do post-sale warning, isn't it foreseeable that employer will not act, and thus arguably some duty by Careful to reach ultimate users?

Will court apply the analog of the learned intermediary rule to a non-medical situation?

Argument for:

"Careful sent information about the safety devices to Beta and also sent accident-preventing warning labels to be affixed to the machine. Identical information was sent each of the next four years."

Argument against:

Foreseeable that company would disregard warnings

Question Copy

Paula had been working at the Beta Plastics Company (Beta) assembly line all day and was looking forward to an evening of bowling. Today's work, making plastic hockey pucks, required that she operate the press twice for each puck. Often the plastic stuck to the top die, and she had to peel the plastic free. Once, as she reached up to free the plastic from the die, she inadvertently hit the activator foot pedal, and the press crushed her hand.

The machine was sold to Beta by Careful Technologies (Careful) fifteen years earlier when there were no industry standards for any safety features. Although the machine Paula was working on had no safety features, Careful had design modifications and safety devices available at the time which would have prevented Paula's injury. Five years after Beta bought the machine, Careful sent information about the safety devices to Beta and also sent accident-preventing warning labels to be affixed to the machine. Identical information was sent each of the next four years. Beta never responded to the letters, nor did it install any of the safety devices or affix the warning labels. Paula sues Careful. What result?

Chapter 5

Multi-Issue Torts Questions

This chapter will focus on organizing and writing answers to multi-party, multi-tort questions. Answers to these questions can be organized either by tort or by party. You should practice writing your answers both ways so that you can determine which approach works best for you under which circumstances.

It is sometimes best not to decide right away whether to organize your answer by tort or by party. One approach you might try is to take notes on a question by party. Make a list of all the parties, and then put on your note sheet every possible combination of parties. Then read the fact pattern sentence by sentence looking for torts to put into the party combination list. Finally, try to think of anything the defendant member of every party combination may have done to the plaintiff. This works for some students, but taking notes by tort may work better for you. If you do organize by parties, and two defendants have similar liability, you can probably incorporate by reference what you said about a given tort when you discuss the second party. But be careful. Sometimes the analysis is similar but not the same. For example, one defendant may be a minor. Or one defendant may be the employer, who is vicariously liable for actions of an employee, and may **also** be liable for negligent supervision or negligently selecting or training of the employee.

You must discuss many items on the professor's score sheet to get your points. The multiple topics in these questions require that you practice under timed conditions beforehand or you won't be able to finish your answers. Only with practice will you know how much detail you can cover in a given amount of time.

In the following variation of a by-now-familiar fact pattern, we have set out every party combination and what we see as the possible torts.

Question

John, the personnel manager, and Jim, a new employee, got onto the elevator at Widget Company at 9:00 a.m. Standing in the front, away from everyone else, was Robert. All the employees of the company knew Robert had an abnormal fear of germs. He never shook hands with anyone. John had just learned that Robert had filed a complaint against him with the company president that John felt was unjustified. He decided to make Robert's life miserable and suddenly reached out to shake Robert's hand. Although Robert recoiled in horror, John grabbed his hand and greeted him heartily. Jim had not paid much attention to John's seemingly harmless behavior and was not paying attention when suddenly Robert shouted, "Take this you bully" and lashed out at John with his umbrella. John ducked, and Robert hit the unsuspecting Jim on the head with the umbrella. Jim was momentarily stunned but not otherwise hurt. He grabbed Robert's umbrella and yanked it away from Robert, to prevent him from now attacking John. Most people on the elevator (including Robert) worked on the 5th floor, so when the elevator stopped there, everyone pushed to get out. When Robert tried to get off the elevator, Jim grabbed him from behind and refused to let him get off. He led him to the security office where a senior guard, who knew of Robert's condition, decided that Robert should be released with a warning. Robert was so upset from the events that he suffered a migraine headache which kept him out of work for two days. Who is liable to whom?

John v. Jim — any claims?

John v. Robert—assault, negligence

Jim v. John—battery, negligence (endangering Jim by his treatment of Robert); (foreseeable reaction? foreseeable plaintiff? legal cause?)

Jim v. Robert—battery, no assault (unless he saw it coming)

Robert v. John—assault, battery, intentional infliction of emotional distress, negligence, (defamation?—depending on what he told the guard)

Robert v. Jim—false imprisonment, battery, assault, possible trespass to chattels

Robert v. senior guard—possible false imprisonment[1]

---

1. Add anything else you can find to this list. Then try writing answers organized by tort ("here are all the possible batteries ...") and by parties. When you organize by party combination, give the complete rule for each tort once. Usually you can say "see above" for any subsequent occurrences (but while that will work for laying out the elements, make sure you make clear for each party combination *how* the element is demonstrated).

Question Copy

John, the personnel manager, and Jim, a new employee, got onto the elevator at Widget Company at 9:00 a.m. Standing in the front, away from everyone else, was Robert. All the employees of the company knew Robert had an abnormal fear of germs. He never shook hands with anyone. John had just learned that Robert had filed a complaint against him with the company president that John felt was unjustified. He decided to make Robert's life miserable and suddenly reached out to shake Robert's hand. Although Robert recoiled in horror, John grabbed his hand and greeted him heartily. Jim had not paid much attention to John's seemingly harmless behavior and was not paying attention when suddenly Robert shouted, "Take this you bully" and lashed out at John with his umbrella. John ducked, and Robert hit the unsuspecting Jim on the head with the umbrella. Jim was momentarily stunned but not otherwise hurt. He grabbed Robert's umbrella and yanked it away from Robert, to prevent him from now attacking John. Most people on the elevator (including Robert) worked on the 5th floor, so when the elevator stopped there, everyone pushed to get out. When Robert tried to get off the elevator, Jim grabbed him from behind and refused to let him get off. He led him to the security office where a senior guard, who knew of Robert's condition, decided that Robert should be released with a warning. Robert was so upset from the events that he suffered a migraine headache which kept him out of work for two days. Who is liable to whom?

You may be faced with a products liability question in which you must discuss all theories of recovery for all parties. The following (a variation on a question in the Strict Liability and Products Liability chapter) is such a question. You must decide whether to organize by party or by legal theory. Although we have set up the notes by party combination, this question probably lends itself better to be organized by legal theory. We have included some sample answer paragraphs as models—these are not complete answers.

Question

Black Motor Company manufactured an automobile that it sold to Cain Cars, a retail dealer, which in turn sold it to Kevin. Kevin bought the car because it was a model that had several years of high rankings by several consumer groups. He was a traveling salesman who depended upon the reliable performance of his car. On his first use of his new car, Kevin drove from his suburban home into the city to meet his fiancée, Melinda, for dinner. There were traffic lights at each intersection so he was not able to go very fast. At one intersection he saw the traffic light facing him turn from green to yellow. He thought he could get across the intersection before the light turned red so he sped up. However, as he got to the pedestrian crosswalk he realized that he couldn't make it through the intersection and applied the brakes. The brakes failed. Kevin steered sharply to the right to avoid the cars that were by now crossing in front of him. The car went onto the sidewalk and hit the building on the corner owned by Mr. Jones, shattering his store window. What are the rights and liabilities of the parties?

Notes for Answer

Kevin v. Black Motor Company

Products liability

Defective condition—brakes failed soon after purchase
(manufacturing defect? Or possibly design defect?)

Commercial supplier—Black Motor Company

When left defendant's control—no change before getting to consumer since no evidence Cain Cars touched the brakes

Foreseeable person injured—Kevin bought the car

Negligence

Implied warranty of merchantability

Kevin v. Cain Cars

Products liability

Negligence—highly unlikely

Implied warranty of merchantability

Mr. Jones v. Black Motor Company

Products liability

Negligence

Implied warranty

Mr. Jones v. Cain Cars

Products liability

Implied warranty of merchantability

Mr. Jones v. Kevin

Negligence

Trespass to land?

Sample Paragraphs

Kevin v. Black Motors[2]

The brakes appear to have been defective—a manufacturing defect.

Since there is no evidence that the product underwent significant changes before reaching Kevin, it seems clear that the brakes were defective when the car left

2. First, you would go through a step-by-step recitation of the elements, and discuss whether each is met. What follows is a partial answer that focuses on a few of the key aspects you should address.

Black's control. The failure of the brakes led to a crash. The crash injured the purchaser of the car—the type of harm and a user who was foreseeable. The defendant is the manufacturer, obviously in the chain of distribution and in the business of manufacturing and selling cars. Black would be liable to Kevin.

Kevin v. Black Motors[3]

Negligence

Negligence requires showing some fault on the part of Black Motors. Often a manufacturing defect involves a company that used a high degree of care—maybe enough for reasonable care—in their manufacturing process. This would negate negligence liability. Of course, Black Motors might have been negligent in inspecting the car before it left the factory; if this defect was detectable upon reasonable inspection, Black breached its duty to Kevin and would be liable in negligence.

Kevin v. Black Motors[3]

Implied warranty of merchantability

In states in which recovery is based on implied warranty of merchantability rather than on strict liability, the rule is that a merchant must sell goods that are merchantable. Merchantable often means "fit for the ordinary purposes for which such goods are used." A car with defective brakes is obviously not fit for the purpose for which a car is used. Therefore, in jurisdictions in which implied warranty is the theory of recovery, Black will be liable to Kevin. The warranty clearly extends to the purchaser.

Mr. Jones v. Black Motors[4]

Products liability

The element at issue here is legal cause.[4] That brake failure would likely result in a car hitting a person or an object would be a strong argument. Most courts would not limit a products liability claim to the narrower class of plaintiffs. Therefore, Mr. Jones would likely have a claim also. The result might be different for an implied warranty claim.

---

3. This is a partial answer that focuses on a few of the key aspects you should address.

4. Present arguments for and against considering this type of injury foreseeable and this plaintiff foreseeable (because the plaintiff is a third party and therefore neither the purchaser of the product nor a member of their family).

Question Copy

Black Motor Company manufactured an automobile that it sold to Cain Cars, a retail dealer, which in turn sold it to Kevin. Kevin bought the car because it was a model that had several years of high rankings by several consumer groups. He was a traveling salesman who depended upon the reliable performance of his car. On his first use of his new car, Kevin drove from his suburban home into the city to meet his fiancée, Melinda, for dinner. There were traffic lights at each intersection so he was not able to go very fast. At one intersection he saw the traffic light facing him turn from green to yellow. He thought he could get across the intersection before the light turned red so he sped up. However, as he got to the pedestrian crosswalk he realized that he couldn't make it through the intersection and applied the brakes. The brakes failed. Kevin steered sharply to the right to avoid the cars that were by now crossing in front of him. The car went onto the sidewalk and hit the building on the corner owned by Mr. Jones, shattering his store window. What are the rights and liabilities of the parties?

The following question appeared in the Strict Liability and Products Liability chapter. Now you should add to your products liability answer the analyses for negligence and the implied warranty of merchantability, and also discuss whether Paula has a potential claim against Beta for negligence.

Question

Paula had been working at the Beta Plastics Company (Beta) assembly line all day and was looking forward to an evening of bowling. Today's work, making plastic hockey pucks, required that she operate the press twice for each puck. Often the plastic stuck to the top die, and she had to peel the plastic free. Once, as she reached up to free the plastic from the die, she inadvertently hit the activator foot pedal, and the press crushed her hand.

The machine was sold to Beta by Careful Technologies (Careful) fifteen years earlier when there were no industry standards for any safety features. Although the machine Paula was working on had no safety features, Careful had design modifications and safety devices available at the time which would have prevented Paula's injury. Five years after Beta bought the machine, Careful sent information about the safety devices to Beta and also sent accident-preventing warning labels to be affixed to the machine. Identical information was sent each of the next four years. Beta never responded to the letters, nor did it install any of the safety devices or affix the warning labels. Paula sues Careful and Beta. What result?

Notes for Answer

Paula v. Careful

Negligence

Products Liability

Implied Warranty

Paula v. Beta

Negligence

Question Copy

Paula had been working at the Beta Plastics Company (Beta) assembly line all day and was looking forward to an evening of bowling. Today's work, making plastic hockey pucks, required that she operate the press twice for each puck. Often the plastic stuck to the top die, and she had to peel the plastic free. Once, as she reached up to free the plastic from the die, she inadvertently hit the activator foot pedal, and the press crushed her hand.

The machine was sold to Beta by Careful Technologies (Careful) fifteen years earlier when there were no industry standards for any safety features. Although the machine Paula was working on had no safety features, Careful had design modifications and safety devices available at the time which would have prevented Paula's injury. Five years after Beta bought the machine, Careful sent information about the safety devices to Beta and also sent accident-preventing warning labels to be affixed to the machine. Identical information was sent each of the next four years. Beta never responded to the letters, nor did it install any of the safety devices or affix the warning labels. Paula sues Careful and Beta. What result?

You saw a variation of the next question in the Negligence chapter:

Question

Janet and Bill were just married. They decided to go on their honeymoon to Snow Woods, one of the best ski resorts in the country. Janet was an expert skier, but Bill had only started skiing when he met Janet two years ago. When they bought their lift tickets, the ticket seller said, "Be glad you weren't here yesterday. Man, was it crowded. We had our busiest day this season." Janet agreed to ski with Bill on the intermediate level trails in the morning and then leave him to go to the advanced level trails in the afternoon. Although there hadn't been much snow, they knew Snow Woods had great snow-making equipment. The first run went well, so they decided to try the next most difficult intermediate trail, the very popular Owl View Trail.

As they approached the middle of the run, Bill suddenly was hit from behind by a novice skier for whom this trail was obviously beyond his capabilities. The skier continued on his way. Bill went sprawling. He screamed in pain as he tried to get up. Janet had been skiing behind Bill to help him improve his form. She immediately started towards Bill. She saw someone they had met the night before at dinner skiing toward them. He was a physician with whom they had spent the evening discussing health care reform. She felt relief, but only momentarily. The physician looked right at Bill and then skied away. Janet arrived at Bill's side when two teenage boys stopped, took off their parkas, and made a sling to carry Bill down the mountain. They didn't do a good job of it, and he slipped out of the sling further damaging his foot. Janet decided to ski to the bottom of the mountain to get help. Suddenly she hit a patch of bare ground and fell. Bill had given her Superior Skis for a wedding present, but they did not disengage from her ski boots as claimed by Superior and she broke her leg. What torts?

Now you should see the relevance of the information about the snow-making equipment and how busy the previous day had been. These are facts that you did not need to use before in analyzing this fact pattern. They relate to the patch of bare ground and Janet's claim against Snow Woods for negligence in maintaining the trail. She also has a products liability claim. These are the claims, along with the torts we have discussed in the Negligence chapter, that should get major attention in your answer. However, this question might also be used by your professor to test your ability to find some less obvious claims. For example, does Bill have a claim in battery (not just in negligence) against the novice skier, using substantial certainty to meet the intent requirement? Depending how your professor has taught this, you might raise the strong likelihood of a novice skier on an intermediate trail hitting someone. Or you might determine that it is probable, but not substantially certain, as your professor has defined that term. This is the sort of judgment that you have to make on any exam, and even more so with multiple issues.

Think twice before raising arguments that stretch the rules too far. You may be tempted to write about the least likely claims first because the others seem too obvious for the professor to be testing you about. This is the wrong approach. Most professors want you to discuss the central issues at the greatest length and only then go to the secondary or less certain issues. You may get an A if you spot the subtler issues, but only if you have found and analyzed the others first.

Question Copy

Janet and Bill were just married. They decided to go on their honeymoon to Snow Woods, one of the best ski resorts in the country. Janet was an expert skier, but Bill had only started skiing when he met Janet two years ago. When they bought their lift tickets, the ticket seller said, "Be glad you weren't here yesterday. Man, was it crowded. We had our busiest day this season." Janet agreed to ski with Bill on the intermediate level trails in the morning and then leave him to go to the advanced level trails in the afternoon. Although there hadn't been much snow, they knew Snow Woods had great snow-making equipment. The first run went well, so they decided to try the next most difficult intermediate trail, the very popular Owl View Trail.

As they approached the middle of the run, Bill suddenly was hit from behind by a novice skier for whom this trail was obviously beyond his capabilities. The skier continued on his way. Bill went sprawling. He screamed in pain as he tried to get up. Janet had been skiing behind Bill to help him improve his form. She immediately started towards Bill. She saw someone they had met the night before at dinner skiing toward them. He was a physician with whom they had spent the evening discussing health care reform. She felt relief, but only momentarily. The physician looked right at Bill and then skied away. Janet arrived at Bill's side when two teenage boys stopped, took off their parkas, and made a sling to carry Bill down the mountain. They didn't do a good job of it, and he slipped out of the sling further damaging his foot. Janet decided to ski to the bottom of the mountain to get help. Suddenly she hit a patch of bare ground and fell. Bill had given her Superior Skis for a wedding present, but they did not disengage from her ski boots as claimed by Superior and she broke her leg. What torts?

Chapter 6

Confronting Your Final Exam

Very few of your law school professors will give you any meaningful feedback during the semester. You are unlikely to have many practice questions or midterm exams. Therefore, you will have little information about how you are expected to respond to exam questions. It is perfectly normal to be scared at the thought that a three- or four-hour exam will determine your grade in a course for which you have given so much of your time and effort. If you have followed the advice in the previous sections of this book and have practiced writing many exam answers, you still need a strategy to ensure that you do your best on the actual final exam.

The thing to remember is that most professors will try to test you on most or all of the topics covered in the course (or at least all of the topics to which significant class time was devoted). So it may be useful to read through the entire exam before starting to answer any question. Using a one-page checklist of topics covered in the course (see the next page for such a checklist) you should try to find where each topic is examined (perhaps in more than one question). You might then write down, beside the item in the checklist, the number of the question in which that topic is covered. You have not yet made any mark on the exam booklet. Usually there still will be topics on your checklist without a question number. Although it may not always be true that all topics are covered on the exam, you should at first assume that they **are** all there, and that you have failed to notice them on the first reading of the exam. There is no need to panic if you don't find a topic or if you see whole sections of questions that you don't fully understand. You will read these questions several more times before you put pen to exam booklet or start keyboarding your answer, and you will often find one or more of those missing topics later.

Since it would be inefficient to test every topic more than once, you can often assume that if you see an issue in one question, it may not appear in another question. Again, there is no hard and fast rule, and sometimes topics **do** appear in more than one question. Usually if this is the case, the topic is a major debatable component of one question and a more minor part of the other (or perhaps a different aspect of the topic is addressed in the second question).

As you look over the exam, you may feel more confident about your ability to answer one question as opposed to the others. Unless the rules forbid it, start with this question. While you are concentrating on the question you feel most confident about, a part of your brain will be ruminating over the other questions. Flashes of insight on those more troublesome questions—perhaps sparked by connections to your mental review as you write your first answer—may come to you.

It is important to take to heart the time suggestion for each question made by the professor. This gives you some indication of the depth of answer and number of issues presented, and disciplines your approach so you do not run short of time to answer a point-rich question.

Since it is likely that your professor will grade you using a score sheet allowing only so many points per issue, your wonderful answer for one question will not make up for slighting another question. After you have determined how much time you have for each question, approach it as you have practiced. Spend about half of the allotted time writing your notes for your answer, crossing out the words you have used, and trying to find topics on your checklist for any sentences you have not used. Rearrange the issues you have found to make the best organized answer. Then write.

Torts Checklist

Intentional torts

- Battery
- Assault
- False imprisonment
- Trespass to land
- Trespass to chattels
- Conversion
- Intentional infliction of emotional distress
- Defenses to intentional torts
  - Self-defense
  - Defense of others
  - Defense of property
  - Consent
  - Discipline
  - Arrest and detention
  - Recapture of chattel

Negligence
- Duty
  - Nonfeasance/failure to act
  - Landowner's duties
- Standard of care
- Breach
- Cause in fact
- Legal (proximate) cause
- Harm
- Defenses to negligence
  - Contributory negligence
  - Comparative negligence
  - Assumption of risk
  - Statute of limitations
  - Preemption

Negligent infliction of emotional distress (direct and bystander)

Strict liability
- Animals
- Abnormally dangerous activities

Products Liability
- Manufacturing defect
- Design defect
- Warning defect
- Defenses to products liability

Other topics your professor may have covered:
- Pre-natal injury
- Defamation
- Loss of consortium/wrongful death
- __________
- __________
- __________

Using Old Exams to Prepare

Although some law schools and some professors provide access to old exams, few provide model answers to those exams. Using those previously-used exams on your own to prepare may not be overly helpful. You have no way of knowing whether you have found the issues the author of the exam question had in mind. Nor can you be sure that you have understood the issues correctly. However, you can use those old exams effectively if you can find a few people who are willing to work with you as a team. Also remember that many of the cases in your casebook, which were used to focus on one particular element, can be used as practice problems, with your goal now being to address all of the elements of the given tort.

Under these circumstances—where you don't know the answer to the practice problem—one helpful method is to assign the same question to everyone in your group. Each member prepares a list of the legal theories he or she spots in the question. Under each legal theory each person identifies what needs to be demonstrated for the theory to apply and the words from the fact pattern he or she used to decide that a given element, sub-element, or factor was demonstrated. When the group meets again, the group members share their insights. What one person doesn't find, another one will. When you have agreed on a list of issues, everyone goes home to write out an answer. When everyone has a written answer, meet again. You can compare the organization of your answers and discuss the difficulties you had in writing out your responses.

As exam time approaches, at least some of your practice should be under timed conditions. If the question you choose to work on is a one-hour question, allow a half-hour to prepare notes for an answer. Then meet and share notes. Next, everyone takes a half-hour to write the answer. If you have only written answers to one-issue fact patterns throughout the semester, you may want to make sure you practice handling some multi-issue questions. Although a multi-issue question is in one sense just a series of single issues, it pays to become familiar with the kind of question you are likely to confront and with organizing the multi-issue answer. You should be able to spot the issues in a long fact pattern, know what needs to be demonstrated for each issue, discern which words are in the fact pattern for what purpose, and have a workable format for an answer. At this point in your exam preparation, your major concern should be to consistently be able to organize and present a step-by-step answer to your professor's complex questions.

This method also works well for policy questions, for which this book cannot prepare you. You and your classmates should be able to list recurring policy arguments and the professor's favorite "buzzwords," and figure out how to organize them as "black letter policy" and use them in your answers. Don't be intimidated by the fact that policy seems totally different than rules and elements. If you properly organize the policy arguments that come up over and over, you'll be ready to mentally go down that list just as you would with the elements of a tort.

Final Thoughts

Throughout this book we've tried to give you suggestions on how you can perform your best on your torts exam. Now it's up to you. Take our methods, adapt them to your own style and that of your professor, and you'll be ready to face that exam with confidence. And remember something else—ultimately, you are trying to learn as much as you can in the most effective way possible, not only to do well on your exam, but because some day there will be a client sitting in front of you with a legal problem. Whether it's a fender-bender or a multi-million dollar case, to your client it will be the most important problem in the world. And you will want to have learned as much as you possibly could when you were in law school to be able to help that client. But for now, we hope you are ready to show all you know on your torts exam. Best of luck!

If you have a comment, particularly on how to improve the next edition of this book, please send an email to hkatz@elon.edu.